ROUTLEDGE LIBRARY EDITIONS: AGRIBUSINESS AND LAND USE

Volume 13

MAN AND NATURAL RESOURCES

T0271404

MAN AND NATURAL RESOURCES

An Agricultural Perspective

SIR CEDRIC STANTON HICKS

Routledge
Taylor & Francis Group

LONDON AND NEW YORK

First published in 1975 by Croom Helm Ltd

This edition first published in 2024
by Routledge
4 Park Square, Milton Park, Abingdon, Oxon OX14 4RN

and by Routledge
605 Third Avenue, New York, NY 10158

Routledge is an imprint of the Taylor & Francis Group, an informa business

British Library Cataloguing in Publication Data
A catalogue record for this book is available from the British Library

ISBN: 978-1-032-48321-4 (Set)
ISBN: 978-1-032-47397-0 (Volume 13) (hbk)
ISBN: 978-1-032-47826-5 (Volume 13) (pbk)
ISBN: 978-1-003-38615-5 (Volume 13) (ebk)

DOI: 10.4324/9781003386155

Publisher's Note
The publisher has gone to great lengths to ensure the quality of this reprint but points out that some imperfections in the original copies may be apparent.

Disclaimer
The publisher has made every effort to trace copyright holders and would welcome correspondence from those they have been unable to trace.

Man and Natural Resources

AN AGRICULTURAL PERSPECTIVE

SIR CEDRIC STANTON HICKS

CROOM HELM LONDON

Croom Helm Ltd,
2-10 St. John's Road London SW11
Reprinted 1976
ISBN: 0-85664-006-9

Printed and bound in Great Britain by
REDWOOD BURN LIMITED
Trowbridge & Esher

CONTENTS

PREFACE

Man's predatory attitude to his environment belongs to the historic period which, compared with the duration of his prehistoric development is negligibly brief.

It may be that man's development of speech, and therefore of abstract thought — his crowning glory — has been the fundamental cause of this ecological divorce.

We have passed very swiftly from a justifying, mechanistic period of scientific thought, into an uncertain period of quantum theory, wave mechanics and indeterminacy.

The organic outlook, so-called by Whitehead, may contain the basis for both a proper appreciation of our place in the ecosphere, and of appropriate measures, at the eleventh hour, to retrieve a balanced relationship.

Any repetitious matter in these chapters is because the material overlaps in its significance and cannot be ignored in one section purely because it has already been referred to in another. It must be examined in 'perspective'.

1. THE HUMAN SITUATION

'The most singular and deepest themes in the history of the Universe and Mankind to which all the rest are subordinate, are those in which there is a conflict between Belief and Unbelief, and all epochs wherein Belief prevails under what form it will, are splendid, heart-elevating and fruitful. All epochs on the contrary, where Unbelief, in what form soever, maintains its sorry victory, should they even for a moment glitter with a sham splendour, vanish from the eyes of Posterity, because no one chooses to burden himself with a study of the unfruitful.'

Goethe

I have borrowed from W. Macniele Dixon both the title of this essay, and the quotation that precedes it. It will be apparent from subsequent essays that I make much of the Second Law of Thermodynamics, since in my view, it exercises a dominant directional influence in the phenomena of the biomass – the total life of the ecosphere. This law of unidirectional tendency to a state of final molecular disorder in the physical universe finds an exception to its operation in the phenomenon of life. Erwin Schroedinger, the mathematical physicist, expressed the view that there were two ways in which orderly events can be produced: the statistical way in which order can be produced from disorder, and the way of the Life process, which produces order from disorder.[1]

The second method depends upon the capacity of the life process in the green leaf or green alga to utilise light quanta of energy from the sun. By doing so, the life process, temporarily in the individual entity and permanently in the type or species, apparently defeats the universal tendency to molecular disorder and death, except by cataclysm. It is difficult to pinpoint anything in the human life of which one can say here is the law in action. The overwhelming similarity one finds is what justifies the comparison with it.

Our inner time clock may be an effect of the steady tendency to molecular disorder; so might the inner need for religion be derived from the operation of a physical law. The universal association of religion with the sanctions of secular laws may not be accidental. The freezing of religions in institutional form may in part spell their ultimate failure because of weakening of their essential dynamic quality. Other human institutions of course, appear to be subject to the same law. Is it the Law of Entropy?

1

Whether or not we can ascribe progress to this law, it is certainly true that scientific perspective is essential if we are to avoid sterile, censorious attitudes as a result of the contemporary spate of dramatic disclosures concerning 'pollution'. Nothing could serve better for this purpose than the following reminder from the pen of Nobel physicist Arthur Compton.

'Our life today differs from our grandfathers' much more than did theirs from the life of 2,000 years before. To dramatise the recent increase in the rate of scientific progress, let us compress the time-scale a millionfold. This means that a year ago the first men learned to use certain odd-shaped sticks and stones as tools and weapons. Speech appeared. Then, only last week someone developed the art of skilfully shaping stones to meet his needs. The day before yesterday, man was sufficiently an artist to use simplified pictures as symbolic writing. Yesterday the alphabet was introduced. Bronze was the metal most used. Yesterday afternoon the Greeks were developing their brilliant art and science. Last mid-night Rome fell, hiding for several hours the values of civilised life. Galileo observed his falling bodies at 8.15 this morning. At 11.00 Faraday's Law of Electro-magnetism was developed, which by 11.30 had given us the telegraph, telephone and incandescent light. At 11.40 X-rays were discovered by Roentgen, followed quickly by radium and wireless telegraphy. Only 15 minutes ago the automobile came into general use. Airmail has been carried for barely 5 minutes, and not until a minute ago have we had world-wide broadcasts in short-wave radio.'

The millionfold compression does much more than dramatise our situation, it brings it within the compass of our understanding. Civilised life is such a brief moment of our total human history that one may well marvel that it has been a successful development in any sense at all. The velocity of technological change, arising from a mechanical, scientific trend of thought is the more important because such changes are seen to be accelerated, if not actually caused by, an economic philosophy in association with double entry book-keeping. These reduce day-to-day human affairs to quantities and measure in the same spirit as that embodied in the mechanical laws of Galileo and Isaac Newton. There is an interesting parallel between the failure of mechanics of these intellectual giants of the Renaissance when applied to atomic physics, and the threat to food production by the application of accountancy economics to agri-business.

Heisenberg, born in 1901, demonstrated that equal initial conditions at atomic and subatomic levels could be followed by different consequences, in contradiction of classical mechanics which claimed

that equal conditions were followed by precisely identical consequences.[2]
Where classical physics failed was in their application to entities in the
microcosm.

Newtonian mechanics have operated with precision in the macrocosm
for just four hours on Compton's time-scale. Heisenberg's life span
cannot even be read on the scale! Should it therefore be a matter for
surprise, that the Principle of Indeterminacy came as a shock to the
established views of physical science, or that its implications are quite
unknown to the general public? The environmental crisis is in no aspect
more important than in relation to food production; a dynamic
biological process being steadily, and in places rapidly, destroyed by the
application to it, of simplistic, quantitative, mechanistic theory,
unrelated to the events in the soil-plant microcosm.

Justus von Liebig (1852) drew attention to certain quantitative
chemical aspects of agriculture. Since then theories, developed in
relation to mechanised industry, have been applied to food production.
The short-term results seemed to confirm the theory, but the long-term
effect has been a steady decline in soil fertility, with the creation of
dust-bowls in the United States, Russia and Australia.

A careful reading of Liebig's writings on agricultural chemistry,
reveals the fallacy. Liebig would be amazed and disappointed to see the
half-truths quoted in his name. As Mark Twain said, 'A half-truth is like
a half-brick — it travels further!'

Francesco Maria Grimaldi (1630-1663) accurately recorded in detail
his observation of the shadow cast by a thin wire, illuminated by a beam
of light emerging from a slit parallel to the wire. He noted that the
main shadow cast by the wire was bordered by three coloured stripes,
both outside and within the main shadow. This discovery not only
antedated Huygen's Wave Theory of Light (1678) and Newton's
Corpuscular Theory, but, had it found a favourable scientific climate
of opinion, it could have been recognised as a demonstration of the
Principle of Indeterminacy — 300 years before Heisenberg! This is
about four hours ago on Compton's time-scale!

Our world outlook might have been different had the implications
of Grimaldi's experiment been realised at the time. The true scientist
is well aware of the limitations of his framework of thought, and it is
inappropriate further to enlarge upon the philosophic significance of
the acceptance of the Uncertainty Principle, by physicists. This is the
world of concepts that cannot be expressed by pictures or models so
favoured by Lord Kelvin. Only mathematical equations describe events
in this world, but, do not attempt to describe the 'substance'. The
'Conquest of Nature' has really been the manipulation of the environment, according to economic rather than scientific rules. The irony is
that Nature includes Man himself!

In our search for ever greater sources of energy, which in the end is political power, technology has conjured out of the mathematical equations of the scientist the means of our own destruction, namely, the atomic and hydrogen bombs.

As the conjurer with the white rabbit distracts attention from his operative hand, so modern 'economic-technology', distracts attention from pending disaster by producing ever new technical developments which appear to offer illimitable largesse. We wish to be deceived, or conjurers would find no market for their prestidigitation. So long as we continue in this state of mind we have no cause to blame governments, industry, commerce, the economists, technologists, or least of all, the scientists. The fault is in ourselves.

How did 'scientific' activity begin? That nature presented an apparent order is obvious to all. The sun rises and sets, the seasons come and go, regularly the associated changes repeat themselves. So, early enough, there appeared a belief in cause and effect. There were of course, great disorders; eathquakes, floods, thunderstorms, but in the main, the regularity encouraged the continual questing of the human mind which always discovered order.

But that order was mechanical. We are now in an age when scientists perceive that the mechanical order is apparent only. The order that we see results from the statistical end result of myriads of molecular and sub-molecular movements. In other words, it is the result of chance, for *all these moving entities influence each other in the production of the final result.* A gas exerts a pressure according to precise laws relating to temperature and other factors, yet, when the number of molecules is reduced to the point where they do not influence each other, their individual movements are seen to be erratic. Furthermore, as the Second Law of Thermodynamics assures us, these movements tend towards ultimate equilibrium and thermal death.

Of one aspect of perspective I am certain, that science and technology are not the *cause* of present environmental destruction. For centuries the Chinese used gunpowder only in fireworks. Moreover, properly used, science and technology will provide the means of escape from our present ills. The economist, who has become the instrument of human greed, is blameworthy only as that instrument.

The by-product of industrial dehumanisation has been the inhumanity of man to man, and involves the individual. The threat to the ecosphere however, is an issue, which involves the survival of the race. This threat has become apparent only within recent times and, because it is associated with both accelerating industrial demand and accelerating growth of population, is the more serious.

In respect to soil fertility and food production the outlook is undeniably gloomy, but a change in economic philosophy could halt or even reverse the trend.

4

REFERENCES

1. Schroedinger, E., *What is Life?*, Cambridge University Press, 1948
2. Heisenberg, W., *Uber Quanten Theoretische Umdeutung Kinematischer und Mechanischer Beziehungen*, Zeitschrift fur Physik, 1905
3. Schroedinger, E., *Is Science a Fashion of the Times?* Selected addresses, trans. James Murphy, W.W. Norton, 1935

READINGS

Ardrey, R., *African Genesis*, Fontana Books, 1961
McNeile Dixson, *Gifford Lectures*, Arnold, 1937

2.   MAN IN THE BIOMASS

'Suppose that we were asked to arrange the following in two categories: Distance, Mass, Electric force, Entropy, Beauty, Melody. I think there are the strongest grounds for placing Entropy alongside Beauty and Melody, and not with the first three.

Entropy is only found when the parts are viewed in association, and it is by viewing or hearing the parts in association, that Beauty and Melody are discerned. All these are features of arrangement. It is a pregnant thought that one of these three associates should be able to figure as a commonplace quantity of science.'

Sir A.S. Eddington, FRS, *The Nature of the Physical World*, 1928.

Between the atmosphere and lithosphere, the gaseous shell surrounding the earth and the solid sphere itself, is the biosphere, that layer occupied by the biomass, the total mass of living things which covers the surface of our planet like mould on a grape. This layer of life, of which our bodies form part, lies at the interface between the atmosphere and the solid and water surfaces of the earth.

The biomass has the capacity to receive and to utilise solar energy in the form of light. This form of energy is the fundamental source of its existence. Light is the key to all life. The great deeps of the oceans are almost barren of life because light is absorbed by the surface waters and does not reach them. Those creatures that do live in the dark abysses owe their existence to those that receive light nearer the surface, their dead bodies sinking down to them providing the energy-rich compounds for sustaining life. It is the same in caves and clefts. For life to exist there must be light. The range of life in the biomass in any particular location is also limited by temperature and moisture. Few living creatures exist or flourish on the edge of hot sulphur springs, polar snow, desert heat, or where moisture is minimal. But everywhere on the earth, with a few extreme exceptions, life has been found to exist, or, to express it another way, the biomass, in varying degrees of thickness and activity, covers the earth's surface where open skies, and water and solid earth make contact.

The biomass is highly diversified, from simple lichens and mosses to giant redwood trees; from bacteria to elephants; and from lice to men. Within the ecosphere, comprising the biomass as a whole, all these myriads of living things interact with each other and with the earth's surface, changing themselves as well as the surface of the earth itself. The coral organism laboriously builds limestone reefs which, on

6

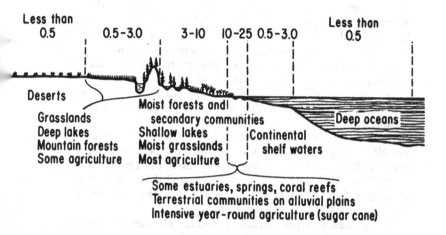

Less than 0.5	0.5-3.0	3-10	10-25	0.5-3.0	Less than 0.5

Deserts
Grasslands
Deep lakes
Mountain forests
Some agriculture

Moist forests and
secondary communities
Shallow lakes
Moist grasslands
Most agriculture

Continental
shelf waters

Deep oceans

Some estuaries, springs, coral reefs
Terrestrial communities on alluvial plains
Intensive year-round agriculture (sugar cane)

Fig 1. *Productivity of different regions of the biosphere, expressed in grams of dry matter per square metre per day (From Odum* Fundamentals of Ecology, *1959, Saunders, Philadelphia.)*

reaching the surface, collect soil-forming flotsam and finally form tropical islands. The lichen, that strange, symbiotic association of plants and fungi, grows on barren rock, even in Antarctica; in temperate climes it lays the foundation for a soil on which will grow first moss, then lowly plants, and finally dense forests.

Within the biosphere, there is constant interaction between its living parts, the population and composition varying with the climate, season, terrain. The study of this interaction reveals a self-regulating system, a multiple form of feed-back effect, operating between all the living things within the system. This system has been called an ecosystem. From a self-regulating standpoint, a biosphere becomes an ecosphere, and the field of study of the ecologist. His interest is in the mode of interrelations which maintain the checks and balances within the system. A subject such as an African national park would interest him, where he would seek to understand the relation between the variety of wild animals and their relative numbers. There are few lions, but

7

countless wildebeest and antelopes. Whatever the composition of mixed animal, fish or bird population, the balance between various types is altered only by climatic or other variations. For a short period conditions may favour one type more than another, but this dynamic balance is the characteristic feature of the ecosphere. If a lush season favours the growth of rabbits, that growth in turn favours an increase of predators, and vice versa.

This equilibrium is the characteristic feature of the ecosphere, even when the usual factors of climate or food are absent. Recently, Krebs and his colleagues studied the population fluctuations of the lemmings and voles at Baker Lake, Canada.[1] The remarkable periodic fluctuations in the populations of these creatures seem unexplained in terms either of predators, or of food availability. The voles and the lemmings speed their rate of breeding and then halt. Formerly it was believed that the increase of lemmings took place when lichen was plentiful and that the astonishing migrations took place when it became depleted.

Workers, like Calhoun and Tustin, think that populations of animals are self-limiting. When recently it was noted that African elephants ceased to breed as their numbers began to assume larger than average proportions, the park rangers naturally concluded that increasing shortage of food resources was the cause, but subsequently decided that it was some other unknown factor.

The biomass therefore, including voles and elephants, functions as an ecosystem. Man is an integral part of the biomass but Western civilised man is no longer part of the ecosystem, because, though he lives on it, he fails to restore his waste material to it.

The undisturbed cycle of the ecosystem continues through the agency of living organisms of all kinds to a final degradation of the waste material into the original simple molecules, which are again recycled within the closed system; the whole activity takes place in aqueous solution. The final degradation stage within the terrestrial sphere occurs in the soil, which is not an inanimate mass of plant nutrients but a complex microcosm of the ecosphere, into which the green-leafed plants extend their roots to absorb the final breakdown products of the living cycles. These very roots themselves, by their excretions into the soil, share their functions with those of the soil micro-organisms and vice versa.

Unfortunately, Western civilisation has distorted the cyclic relationship between man and his ecosystem. The following diagrams compare the conditions in an intact natural ecosystem with those of a degraded (rough grazing) and an artificial agricultural ecosystem.

The diversity of living things in a natural ecosystem is well seen in Fig. 2. The greater the diversity, the more stable is the system in

8

Fig 2. *Energy cycles of the biosphere are powered by the sun. Land plants bind solar energy into organic compounds (heavy broken arrows) utilised successfully by herbivores, carnivores, and scavengers; residual compounds are decomposed by bacteria (light solid arrows). Energy is fixed by microscopic sea plants through a similar 'food chain' (heavy solid arrows). In the water cycle (light broken arrows) water evaporated from the sea is precipitated on land and used by living organisms, and eventually returns to the sea bearing minerals and organic matter. (From Cole,*Scientific American, *April 1958.)*

9

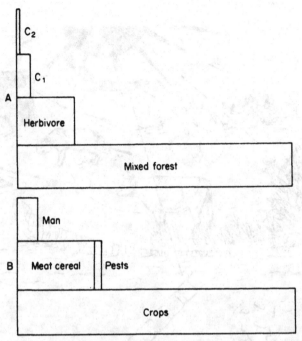

Fig 3. *Represents the relationship between the natural ecosystem, e.g. mixed forest, and the population of herbivores and primary and secondary carnivores comprising the food chain.*

Fig 4. *Illustrates the artificial relationship established by advanced technological agriculture. Monoculture is the rule. There is little diversity in the ecosystem.*

the face of climatic change. Those creatures which become pests in our Western type of systems are kept in balance in a natural ecosystem.

An ecosystem has a metabolism of its own. There is an input, output, and turnover of both materials and energy, as in an animal body, and the soil is an important element. J.H. Quastel,[2] a distinguished biochemist, was the first to study, quantitatively, the metabolism of the soil. More ambitiously, Howard Odum[3] has made studies of entire ecosystems. His diagram (Fig.5) depicts ecocycles of both a terrestrial grassland, and an associated pond.

If there exists a balance between plant, animal, insect and microbial populations in a natural ecosystem then there will be a balanced transfer of energy throughout the system. Field studies show that approximately 10-20 per cent of energy is available for transfer from plants to grazing animals, and a further 10-20 per cent from grazing animals to carnivores, and so on, for at least some four levels of carnivore population. The last level contains the largest animals. The cycle is completed by the chain of decomposition: leaf- and bark-fall,

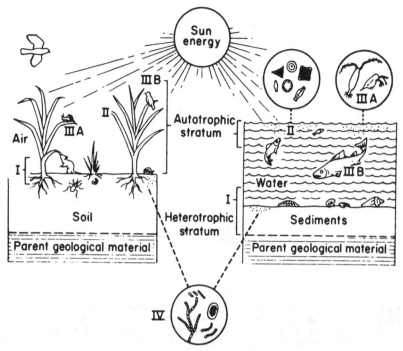

Fig 5. *Correspondence of components of terrestrial (left) and aquatic (right) ecosystems. I = abiotic components, II = photoautotrophs, IIIA = primary consumers, IIIB = secondary consumers, IV = decomposers. (After Odum,* Ecology, *Holt, Rinehart & Winston, Inc., New York, 1963)*

rotting branches and fallen trees, excreta, dead plants and animals. Efficient as these cycles are, dangerous consequences follow if toxic materials are introduced at any point for the following reasons.

Any persistent, potentially toxic agent collected by plants or animals at the commencement of a food chain will be concentrated at each step in the next predator along the chain. The diagram redrawn after Woodwell,[4] illustrates these two aspects of the biomass, namely, the diminishing number of individuals, or quantity of life, at each 10 to 20 per cent energy transfer, and the corresponding increase in individual size as well as in concentration of a toxic agent.

Let us consider some examples.

In Sweden, fishing is now forbidden in certain of the largest lakes, because of the high concentration of mercury compounds in the flesh of the largest and most desirable fish. Victoria, in Australia, has recently stopped the sale of school shark for the same reason.

The mercury was discharged in its metallic form from caustic soda plants into streams and lakes. The metallic mercury was harmless, being insoluble, but a bacterium living in bottom mud converted the mercury

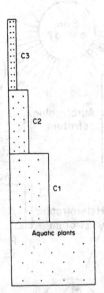

Fig 6. *As the biomass diminishes in passing along a food chain from aquatic plants to plant carnivores 1, 2 and 3, the concentration of a toxic pesticide e.g. D.D.T. increases. At each step in the food chain, diminution of biomass is due to losses in metabolism (an aspect of increasing entropy). The pesticide however is not excreted or metabolised at a comparable rate. Rivers and lakes are extensively polluted with pesticides carried in run-off from farms, orchards and aerial spraying.*

into an organic compound within itself; the presence of the bacterium was due to contamination of the water by raw sewage. Animalcules consumed them; and, in their turn, small fish consumed the crustacea. Larger and desirable edible fish consumed the minnows, and finally man received the concentrated dose. Not for many years, was this mystery elucidated, until the cause of strange mental symptoms in young people was sought.

Metallic mercury has long been known to be poisonous under limited conditions where its vapour could be inhaled in a confined space, or where it came into continual contact with the skin. Its soluble compounds have always been recognised as dangerous; now, metallic mercury has emerged as a menace to industrial populations.

Toxic mercury accumulation in a food chain was first suspected in Japan. Between the years 1954 and 1960 some 111 persons were killed by eating shellfish contaminated with methyl-mercury, due to pollution by the effluent from a chemical industry producing vinyl chloride and acetaldehyde. Since this occurrence at Minamata, a further 26 people died from a similar cause at Ningata in 1965. The Swedes

12

showed that methyl-mercury persists in the human body for 140 days after ingestion, with a 'half-life' of 70 days. Thus, if a further amount of the same quantity be consumed after that period, it is added to the amount still remaining in the body. This means that methyl-mercury is a cumulative poison, and that a toxic level of 0·2 micrograms per gram of blood would be reached in a man weighing 150 lbs after a daily consumption of 300 micrograms.

The Swedish Natural Science Research Council has established the maximum daily 'safe' intake of methyl-mercury at one-tenth of this quantity for an adult, 30 micrograms daily. For children, the intake would be correspondingly less. Dr Grimstone,[5] of Merton College, Oxford, has estimated that the mercury intake from foods other than fish, is approximately 30 micrograms per person per week in the United Kingdom. If this is the case, about 2 oz of fish would be a permissible weekly intake, assuming that 20 micrograms is in the form of methyl-mercury.

The signs of mercury poisoning are due to the action of methyl-mercury on specific areas of the brain. They are unsteady gait, blurring and limitation of vision, deafness, and numbness of the fingers and toes. Moreover, there is a curious inability on the part of a poisoned person to conduct an intelligent conversation with more than one person at a time. This had been interpreted in Sweden, prior to recognition of the cause, as indicating some form of mental disability.

Personality disturbances have also been traced to chronic mercury poisoning: excessive self-consciousness and embarrassment, timidity, anxiety and indecision, inability to concentrate, irritability associated with despondency or depression and resentment of criticism. All these may slowly appear with finally, complete change of personality. There are obvious difficulties over diagnosis of the condition from such vague symptoms.

Not all mercury found in sea fish originates from industrial pollution. A low mercury level of 0·01-0·1 milligrams per kilo is found in fish from uncontaminated areas. It has been suggested that submarine volcanic activity, known to occur in the seabed, is responsible. Analysis of 1,000-year-old fishbones has revealed similar amounts of mercury and of tuna fish caught between 1878 and 1909 and preserved at the Smithsonian Institute in Washington, similar amounts.

Tuna and swordfish are at the apex of the food chain and can concentrate even the naturally occurring mercury of the sea to harmful levels for human food.

For the British Isles, the highest values for mercury in fish are found in catches from the Irish Sea, particularly from the region of Morecambe Bay, where there is pollution from chlorine alkali works. Since mercury is a valuable metal, it is surprising how wasteful is the operation of the

13

Kastner-Kellner process for manufacturing caustic soda and chlorine. The Dow Chemical Company of Canada, for example, discovered a loss of some 30 lbs of metallic mercury daily, that had been continuing for 20 years![6] Another metallic toxic agent of importance is lead. Chronic lead poisoning has been a human hazard from at least Greek and Roman times. The Romans customarily used lead water-pipes, cisterns, wine vessels and dishes, while the Greeks had long before recorded their diagnosis of lead poisoning. Tanqueril in 1830 was the first to describe the mental disturbance resulting from lead poisoning which he called lead encephalopathy. All those trades where lead dust was created, or workmen's hands became ingrained with lead (and these were legion), were liable to produce chronic poisoning. However, in England, it was not until the turn of the century that public health industrial legislation aimed to remove these hazards. The literature on lead poisoning from the metal, not its salts, is surprisingly large, and ranges from such topics as contamination of foods from the solder of food cans to the use of lead foil wrapping, and lead pipes to carry beer.

As in the case of mercury poisoning, a new *organic* compound of lead has become involved in pollution. This substance is lead tetraethyl, a chemical cousin of methyl-mercury, widely used as an anti-knock additive in petrol for use in high compression internal combustion engines. Poisoning by the additive itself results mostly from industrial exposure, as when leaded petrol is used for degreasing. The main hazard to the general public is the emission of lead oxide in the form of an aerosol, in the fumes of motor-car exhausts.

The Medical Research Council air pollution unit found 10 per cent of the airborne lead in Fleet Street, London, during heavy traffic, to be in the organic form.[7] The air of cities of the United Kingdom quite often contains more than 2·7 micrograms per cubic metre during twenty-four hours. The U.S. Government Environmental Protection Agency has officially stated that an average atmospheric concentration of lead exceeding 2 micrograms per cubic metre for periods of three months or more is a hazard to public health. In the U.S.S.R., the maximum atmospheric concentration that is permitted is 0·7 micrograms per cubic metre.

A common early symptom of chronic lead poisoning is insomnia, and results of animal experiments appear to confirm this early cerebral effect. The astronomical rise in the use of sleeping tablets, relaxants and tranquillisers in the United States and the United Kingdom may be in part due to lead in the urban atmosphere.

Although these facts are well known, governments have been slow to act on the health hazards of exposure to such levels of atmospheric contamination by inorganic and organic lead compounds. As Rice-Smith emphasises in his article on Chemistry in Britain of June 1972, children, pregnant and nursing mothers and sufferers from neuroses or psychopathic disturbance may be at even greater risk, since the central nervous system of the child is much more sensitive to lead poisoning. He draws attention to some disturbing facts and figures.

'The daily ingestion of 800-1,000 micrograms of lead by a young child over a period of several months can produce clinical lead poisoning. Dietary levels below this should obviously be regarded with suspicion particularly when reinforced by inhalation of airborne lead, ingestion of tube paint, etc. This potentially toxic intake is provided by 1 lb of food at United Kingdom statutory maximum of 2 parts per million (up to 5 parts per million of canned meat).'

Thompson recently found a range of 70-750 micrograms of lead 'in the normal daily diet of 5 adults not especially exposed to lead at work or by accident.'

Evidently therefore, even without the ingestion of any airborne lead, the child may be exposed to possible low grade poisoning manifested by disturbed behaviour or impaired development of the intellect, which can occur without obvious signs of ill health.

So long ago as 1943 there appeared in a leading paediatric journal the results of a ten-year clinical study of 20 children supposedly cured of lead poisoning. The children's ages ranged from 10 months to 11 years. Their lead poisoning had not been severe, and only 8 had shown any signs of mental disturbance. When discharged from hospital they had been without any symptoms or signs. Nevertheless, in only one of these children was the subsequent mental development quite normal. The remaining 19 demonstrated measurable and identifiable abnormalities, such as dyslexia where the subject can identify the letters of the alphabet, but cannot put them together to make words, and therefore is unable to read. There was also loss of inhibitory functions of the brain, leading to impulsive behaviour, and sometimes violence. One 11-year-old child was returned to hospital with severe behavioural and educational difficulties, because it was suspected that a new mobilisation of lead from the bones might be the cause. This suspicion seemed confirmed when treatment again 'cured' the disturbances, and the child returned to school where her progress was normal but only fair.

Since this study was published confirmatory investigations have led to the general conclusion that mild lead poisoning leaves some 25 per cent of survivors with permanent brain damage. A second episode of poisoning will result in almost 100 per cent damage. Byers and Lord[8] in their original paper of 1943 concluded that an unanswered question remained to plague them. Is a child with elevated levels of lead in the blood, though without symptoms of lead poisoning, subject to

15

brain damage in the long term? If so, the implications for our younger generation are grave indeed.

Recent surveys in cities of Britain reveal blood lead levels of 0·4 parts per million with some reaching double that value. Levels of 0·3-0·5 p.p.m. are considered undesirable, and 0·8 p.p.m. indicates the imminence of encephalopathy. An American study shows that in four areas, 25 per cent of children have absorbed potentially dangerous quantities of lead, and up to 5 per cent have acute clinical symptoms.

Are these findings of high blood lead levels a sign of chronic lead poisoning, and if so, does this point to a contributory cause of behavioural disorders in urban society? A report of the National Academy of Sciences makes the point that childhood attacks of symptomatic lead poisoning can produce 'hostile, aggressive and destructive behaviour patterns'. The *Swiss Medical Journal* (1971) reports blood lead levels between 0·405 and 0·433 in the inmates of two reformatories. This is surely an interesting example of correlation between blood chemistry and abnormal behaviour, and one deserving of further study. Atmospheric pollution added to the extensive sources of lead in food could well prove to be the 'last straw that breaks the camel's back'.

It is significant that over the period 1960-68, although the quantity of lead per 100,000 gallons of petrol remained relatively constant, the consumption of lead additives rose almost 70 per cent and the average miles per gallon fell 7 per cent. This was the clear result of an increase in the number of motor vehicles on the road and in their average horse-power.

In addition to lead, the internal combustion engine is responsible for the considerable pollution from carbon monoxide. This gas combines with the haemoglobin of the blood to form a very stable compound which lowers both the amount of oxygen the blood can carry and the rate at which it is delivered to the body tissues, thus depriving the brain and nerve cells of the very high oxygen pressure level they require for efficient functioning. As motorists commonly smoke cigarettes while driving more carbon monoxide is added to the blood, resulting in the particularly high concentration of it in congested traffic.

Having seen how the concentration of contaminants may increase during transfer through the ecosystem, we must now turn to the opposite process and see how the complex molecules of life and the energy available decreases at every step. This metabolism or turnover, both by individual organisms, and by the biomass as a whole in its ecosystems, poses a deep philosophic question.

The living phenomenon of metabolism attracted the attention of Erwin Schroedinger, a great mathematical physicist. In a series of lectures delivered at Trinity College, Dublin, in 1943, under the title 'What is Life?', he developed the idea that life was a manifestation of certain very large and relatively stable complex molecular systems whose architecture apparently resisted the universal physical tendency to molecular disorder, the final stages of which is dissolution and death. Final molecular disorder is a state of maximum entropy, when there is no flow of energy from one region to another. (The term entropy was introduced by Rudolph Clausius in 1850.) Any physical system can be described in terms of its entropy. A coiled spring, or a boulder poised on a cliff edge has less entropy compared with the uncoiled state of the spring or the fallen boulder. Thus, the Second Law of Thermodynamics is the law of probability or chance. When it was described in such terms by Ludwig Boltzman in 1896 there arose a philosophical storm that lasted into this century. For the first time physics was faced with a unidirectional tendency in nature, ultimate thermal death, which was repugnant to the world outlook of the period. In the early years of the nineteenth century it was believed that if everything possible was known about a cause, an effect could be confidently predicted; now all was reduced to probability. This has finally become the basic approach to the study of energy changes. Darwin's theory of evolution by natural selection of types more adaptive to the environment also emphasised the influence of chance, and, with Boltzman's contribution to physics, enhanced the trend away from traditional religious belief.

Let us now return to our green leaf and green alga with their chloroplasts, and to the capture and flow of energy. The chloroplasts capture energy in the packaged form of light quanta or photons, and utilise it in electron cycles to construct energy-rich compounds, which in turn drive the living systems of these organisms. This process of photosynthesis involves decrease of entropy and diminishing energy. The cycle of exchange closes after complete decay, but the hairs of the plant roots, or the algae in an aqueous system, again driven by solar energy, recycle the elementary molecules, restoring the energy and order, and so on, *ad infinitum.* Without light energy from outside, there would be no such cycle of change. However this process is slowed down or prevented; ageing inevitably brings it to its conclusion. Just what part is played in the system by reproduction and the exchange of genes is as yet not understood.

This brief diversion clarifies the reason for diversity in any natural ecosystem: the flow of energy and material offers manifold niches for a highly heterogeneous population of living things, both for those that require a longer stretch of 'the river', and those that can manage with the energy available from a minor 'backwater'. The common blowfly, for example, can extract adequate 'negative entropy' – to use

Schroedinger's term — from the excrement of higher animals. The bacteria and protozoa of decay can and do extract the last available 'negative entropy' from the final debris of dead organisms before joining the debris themselves.

Turning back to Odum's ecological diagram of field and pond, we can reconsider the question posed by Schroedinger. The diversity of living things is only one aspect of the ecosphere; there is another that is less obvious owing to diversity, the biomass can adjust itself to changing conditions. Some living things form a major proportion, others a minor or even minute proportion of the biomass, because populations of given species vary in the course of time. The biomass is a heterogeneous *quantity* of living things, and life within the biomass presses always against its limits, whatever they may be.

Odum again has studied the regeneration of abandoned farmland in the south-east of the USA.

There is an obvious succession of living things as regeneration proceeds (regeneration in this sense means reoccupation of the biosphere by the optimum biomass). At first only grasshoppers (primary heterotrophs) feed on the mixed pastural herbage (primary autotrophs), and insectivorous birds (secondary heterotrophs) feed upon the grasshoppers. As the physical and chemical conditions change owing to ecological interactions (soil population of micro-organisms and availability of plant foods), plants and animals also change. Ground birds are replaced by tree nesters; new insects related to bark, leaf, leaf-fall appear.

It has been well established that such regeneration always follows a regular succession, indicating the existence of regulatory systems of feed-back within the biomass, and between the biomass and the biosphere, including rainfall — both quantity and pattern — temperature range, wind velocity and so forth. It is this diversity within the biomass that makes both for stability and for adjustment to changes in the biosphere.

Just as the biomass acting as an ecosystem has adjusted to change on this scale, it has done so on the time scale of palaeontology, where natural selection has favoured the development of mutations more efficient in their utilisation of the energy available in the ecosystem.

The biomass has a long history, on present evidence, at least some three billion years after its beginning as a very thin bacterial film. Photosynthesis appears to have begun two billion years ago, according to dating of the recent finds of fossil traces of blue-green algae in the Gunflint Chert formation of Ontario. With the development of photosynthesis, oxygen began to accumulate in the atmosphere, and new types, able to utilise oxygen began slowly to emerge. Within the last 750 million years, the metazoa (multi-cellular organisms) appeared,

18

Time in years	1–10	10–25	25–100	100+
Community type	Grassland	Shrubs	Pine forest	Hardwood forest

Grasshopper sparrow
Meadowlark
Field sparrow
Yellowthroat
Yellow-breasted chat
Cardinal
Towhee
Bachman's sparrow
Prairie warbler
White-eyed vireo
Pine warbler
Summer tanager
Carolina wren
Carolina chickadee
Blue-gray gnatcatcher
Brown-headed nuthatch
Wood pewee
Hummingbird
Tufted titmouse
Yellow-throated vireo
Hooded warbler
Red-eyed vireo
Hairy woodpecker
Downy woodpecker
Crested flycatcher
Wood thrush
Yellow-billed cuckoo
Black and white warbler
Kentucky warbler
Acadian flycatcher

	1–10	10–25	25–100	100+
Number of common species*	2	8	15	19
Density (pairs per 100 acres)	27	123	113	233

*A common species is arbitrarily designated as one with a density of 5 pairs per 100 acres or greater in one or more of the 4 community types.

Fig 7. *The general pattern of secondary succession on abandoned farmland in the southeastern United States. The upper diagram shows four stages in the life form of the vegetation (grassland, shrubs, pines, hardwoods); the bar graph shows changes in passerine bird population that accompany the changes in autotrophs. A similar pattern will be found in any area where a forest is climax, but the species of plants and animals that take part in the development series will vary according to the climate or topography of the area. (From Odum,* Ecology, *Holt, Rinehart & Winston, Inc., New York, 1963.)*

and later the land plants. Man, as such, is a relative newcomer to the biomass — possibly 3-5 million years ago.

Modern man, that is agricultural man, came on the scene some 10-12 thousand years ago, and appears in the archaeological record at Jarmo and other sites in the so-called 'fertile crescent', where the River Tigris brushes the north-east hills between Baghdad and Mosul in Iraq. More recent finds on the Burma-Thailand border may extend this date by 1,000 years, but more importantly, they disclose the fact that agricultural techniques had, at that distant date, developed in widely separated geographical regions. We may assume therefore, that some 10,000 years ago, man was becoming settled in communities and living from the local soil rather than from hunting and food gathering. This was the decisive moment for the ecosphere so far as man is concerned when the recycling of his wastes became a practical and social problem, and not an ecological procedure.

REFERENCES

1. Krebs, J.B., *Science Journal*, 1963
   —— Ecological Monographs, 36, 1966
2. Quastel, J.H., *Soil Metabolism*, Roy. Inst. Chem., London, 1946
3 Odum, H., *Fundamentals of Ecology*, Saunders, 1959
4. Woodwell, G.M., *The Biosphere*, Sci. Am. Pub., Freeman, 1970
5 Grimstone, G., *Chemistry in Britain*, 1972
6. Ontario Water Commission, *Industrial Water Survey of Dow Chem. Coy.*, 1969
7. Thomson, J.A., *Brit. Journ. Indust. Med.*, 1971
9 Byers, and Lord, E.E., *Am. J. Diseases of Children*, 1943; Lob, M., and Restaunes, P., *Schweiz. med. Wochenschrift*, 1971

READINGS

Grobstein, C., *The Strategy of Life*, Freeman, 1964
—— *The Biosphere*, Sci. Am. Pub., Freeman, 1970

3. INTER FAECES ET URINAM NASCIMUR

When Svetaketu was twelve years old he was sent to a teacher, with whom he studied until he was twenty-four. After learning all the Vedas, he returned home full of conceit in the belief that he was consummately well-educated, and very censorious.

His father said to him, 'Svetaketu, my child, you who are so full of your learning and so censorious, have you asked for that knowledge by which we hear the unhearable, by which we perceive what cannot be perceived, and know what cannot be known?'

'What is that knowledge, Sir?' asked Svetaketu. His father replied: 'As by knowing one lump of clay, all that is made of clay is known, the difference being only in name, but the Truth being all that is clay — so, my child, is that knowledge, knowing which we know all.'

'But, surely, these venerable teachers of mine are ignorant of this knowledge, for if they possessed it they would have imparted it to me. Do you, Sir, therefore, give me this knowledge?'

'So be it,' said the father . . . And he said, 'Bring me a fruit of the Nyagrodha tree.'

'Here is one, Sir.'

'Break it.'

'It is broken, Sir.'

'What do you see there?'

'Some seeds, Sir, exceedingly small.'

'Break one of these.'

'It is broken, Sir.'

'What do you see there?'

'Nothing at all.'

The father said, 'My son, that subtle essence which you do not perceive there — in that very essence stands the being of the huge Nyagrodha tree. In that which is the subtle essence, all that exists has itself. That is the True, that is the Self, and thou, Svetaketu, art That.'

'Pray, Sir,' said the son, 'Tell me more.'

'Be it so, my child,' the father replied; and he said, 'Place this salt in water, and come and see me tomorrow morning.'

The son did as he was told.

Next morning the father said, 'Bring me the salt which you put in the water.'

The son looked for it, but could not find it; for the salt, of course, had dissolved.

The father said, 'Taste some of the water from the surface of the vessel. How is it?'

'Salty.'

'Taste some from the middle, – how is it?'

'Salty.'

'Taste some from the bottom. How is it?'

'Salty.'

The father said, 'Throw the water away and then come back to me again.'

The son did so; but the salt was not lost, for salt exists forever.

The father said, 'Here likewise in this body of yours, my son, you do not perceive the True; but there in fact it is. In that which is the subtle essence, all that exists has itself. That is the True, that is the Self, and thou, Svetaketu, art That.'

From the Chandogya Upanishad. ? 1000 B.C.

We are all aware that, so far as our material bodies are concerned, we live by taking in 'food', and excreting 'waste products.' Food, for the great urban populations of the Western world, means a variety of edible items purchased with money at some shop or other. Only where markets still exist, does the purchaser occasionally come into contact with the man who grows the foodstuffs, so far is metropolitan man removed from the soil that sustains him. Nevertheless, looking beyond the coloured packages, and the meretricious sales gimmicks, we realise that we are, in some mysterious way, part and parcel of those remote pastures, arable fields, and orchards. We are literally what we eat, but, and here is the rub, why must we continue to eat and to excrete? The more sophisticated among us will reply, 'To take in fuel for energy, and to replace "wear and tear".'

Yet, in another sense our bodies are merely a temporary, organised disturbance in a stream of water carrying the nutrients which are derived from the ingested foodstuffs by the processes of digestion. Consider then the composition of the common foodstuffs on which we live. How much is solid matter?

% WATER

Meat 53-65%	Eggs 74%
Fish 79-81%	Bread 37%
Milk 69%	Cereal 8-12%
Cheese 39-74%	Greens 81-93%
Butter 16%	Fruit 80-92%

With the exception of butter (or margarine) and cereal, most foodstuffs consist largely of water. Even the potato is a beverage comparable on the basis of its solid content, with fish. Evidently even before we drink tea, coffee, cocoa or beer, we have already taken in much water in our food.

The quantities of water ingested have been measured under various climatic conditions. An average adult in a mild climate ingests 1,500 c.c. of water, plus 1,000 c.c. in his food daily, and in addition, produces a further 300 c.c. of water from the metabolism of the nutrients. He excretes 1,500 c.c. as urine, and the remainder in the faeces, in the form of sweat, and through the lungs in the expired air. The figure below illustrates the intake and output of a 70 kg man (196½ lbs) doing moderate physical work.

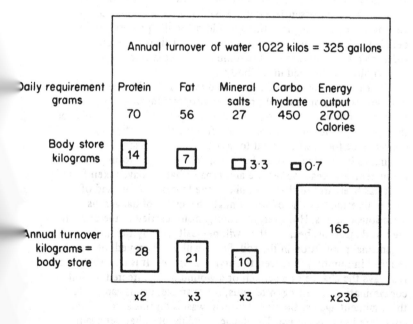

Fig 8.

At a glance it is clear that a stream of water passes through the human body at the rate of at least half a gallon daily. Each adult excretes into the sewerage system at least 1,600 c.c. or one-third gallon of water daily. In this excrement we reject approximately 1 oz of calcium phosphate, and 1¼ oz of soluble, nitrogen-rich material, measured in the dry form. The annual turnover becomes impressive; 10 kilos of mineral salts containing 3 or 4 kilos of phosphate (approx. 7 lbs) together with the soluble nitrogenous residues of 28 kilos of protein, which amounts approximately to 22 lbs of urea. This represents a useful quantity of valuable plant nutrients, which came from the fields, but goes into the rivers and the sea — except in those few instances where sewage treatment and retrieval as manure take place.

Other facts can be ascertained from the diagram. The annual turnover of water is twenty times that of the water content of the body; the protein turnover only twice that amount. The turnover of mineral salts, mainly calcium in the form of phosphate, is three times that of the body's stock, and the carbohydrate two hundred and thirty-six times that of the carbohydrate content of the body. This is of interest for two reasons. Carbohydrates are the source of energy for muscles, heart and more subtle requirements, but the foostuffs containing them are the carriers of the essential vitamins, which are the corner-stones of enzymes; without enzymes there would be no life process, while deficiency leads to malnutrition and disease. This is therefore, a *vulnerable turnover*, despite the minuteness of the fixed store of carbohydrate contained in the body.

The careless way in which urbanised man diverts his stream of nutrients is a major cause of present environmental troubles. It produces pollution on the one hand, and depletion of soil fertility on the other. Furthermore, urbanisation favours the use of processed convenience foods which tend to lack essential accessory factors, leading to lowered vitality and stamina. We no longer form part of the ecosystem, and cease to restore and repay what we have taken from it.

It has been argued that the bulk of the faeces is comprised of bacterial residues, some of which might be agents of dangerous infectious diseases. However, micro-organisms carried in the excrement are not dangerous, because they will be dealt with by the micro-organismal population in the soil. Some will be destroyed, others reduced in number, or forced to survive as spores. It is true that there is always the chance of a scratch or a wound being infected by soil contamination, resulting in tetanus, for example, or gas gangrene, but the argument against the use of human wastes on this account must be considered in perspective. The danger is miniscule when set against the background of ecological destruction resulting from man's separation from his ecosystem.

This separation breaks the cycle and is associated with a new source of pollution by artificial fertilisers, used to compensate for the failure to recycle human waste. These products of the chemical industry do not restore soil fertility; they rather erode it, and, whilst in the short run increasing production albeit by diminishing increments, they also increase pollution of surface waters by nitrate and phosphate. The damage caused in the first place by breaking the re-cycling process, is thus continually aggravated, helped also by the rapid increase in population, as well as urbanisation.

Inefficient disposal of excreta can be extremely dangerous, as we shall see in the next chapter.

READINGS

Gerard, R., *Food for Life*, Chicago University Press, 1952
Hardin, G., *Biology, Its Principles and Implications*, Freeman, 1966

4. DOWN TO EARTH

'A little learning is a dangerous thing,
Drink deep or taste not the Pierian Spring.
These shallow draughts intoxicate the brain,
And drinking largely sobers it again.'

Alexander Pope, *Essays in Criticism*

'Dr. Johnson, you smell!'
'Pardon me, Madam. You smell, I stink!'

Our agricultural forebears had long since learned that human and animal excrement and farm waste had valuable fertilising properties. It was surely an empirical observation, but nevertheless it was an ecological discovery.

With the growth of towns arose the problem of collection and disposal of garbage and excrement. In London during the twelfth century, this was achieved by each dwelling having a refuse pit which was emptied by nightmen, who carried the mess to lay-stalls outside the city walls. These middens were emptied by peasants who carted the material away for application to their fields.

The cobbled streets were constructed with a central channel to carry off rainwater as well as household slops, which were as often as not emptied from an upstairs window with the warning cry 'Garde l'eau'. The citizens were required to keep the pavement and channel in front of their dwellings clean, and the little piles of filth were removed by men called muck-rakers. Today, 'muck-raker' is a term applied to a scandalmonger.

A large number of latrines overhung the River Thames, which, in those pre-embankment days, receded some 200 yards in places. The Strand, at that time, verged on the mudflats. The scene needs no description, nor does the odour! The Master of the Temple was obliged by statute to maintain one of these latrines for free public use. The Wallbrook was lined by one long street of latrines, for the use of which the public paid one shilling per annum.[1]

The year 1307 is memorable, because the stink of the River Fleet reached such a crescendo that a Commission was established to purify the stream. Incense in the neighbouring churches had become inadequate to cope, and ships could not enter the waterway because of the accumulated filth! The Aberdeen inlet at Kowloon in Hong Kong

at low tide provides a modern demonstration of this state of affairs. Although there were from time to time similar Statutory attempts to deal with local situations, it was not until the years 1531-43 and 1601 that successive attempts at regulation extended as far as two miles outside the inner city. By the year 1800, sewers emptying into the Thames carried stormwater only. Cesspools collected excrement, and garbage heaps the decaying vegetable and other matter in the yard of each dwelling. The privy stood over the cesspool, which was still emptied by the nightman, and the garbage by the garbage man.
The well-to-do had their fancy commodes (made by Spode), which the serving wench emptied into the cesspool. The term 'menial' derived from this unpleasant occupation.

The year 1810 saw the introduction of the water-closet, and the invention of that chaste hieroglyph that was to conquer all languages — the W.C. This was slow to be adopted, but, within twenty years was in general use, and with it came a new problem. The W.C. emptied into the cesspool, which overflowed into open channels emptying into the stormwater sewers! These drains in turn emptied into the Thames, which soon became a Brobdingnagian open sewer, leaving at low tide vast, unsavoury stretches of mudflats. By the year 1834 there were ten separate Boards of Commissioners of Sewers within a ten-mile radius of the centre of London. Each had separate and independent jurisdiction, some under Acts of 1531! Regulations differed widely from district to district. Slowly the water-closets were connected to the sewers, but no-one was compelled to drain his dwelling. The death rate rose to between 38-60 per thousand, depending on the congestion of living conditions. While Holborn and Finsbury sewers were enlarged, City sewers were not, so that every heavy fall of rain inundated with sewage the houses nearer the river!

Cesspits still remained in Cheapside and Leadenhall Street, and the fluid contents percolated into the gravel beds from which the water supply was drawn.

In 1834 a certain John Martin, an artist of some distinction, suggested that instead of being allowed to contaminate the river, the sewage should be intercepted by large connecting sewers running along the banks of the Thames. These sewers should be covered by embankments which would have the effect of narrowing the stream and increasing its tidal scouring action. The intercepting sewers should empty further down the stream, away from the densely populated areas.

Despite the ravages of cholera in 1832, the public was not ready for such a proposal, and official opposition was strong. In 1845, Thomas Wickstead, Engineer for the East London Waterworks Company, endeavoured to revive Martin's plan, proposing to extend the outfall to Barking Creek, and to 'deodorise' the sewage. That same year

J.J. Norwood proposed in Parliament plans for using low-lying tunnels on each river bank but without embankment. Neither scheme was accepted, nor was Norwood's proposal when put forward again in 1848.

In the same year all sewage authorities (excepting that of the City) were consolidated in one Board. Twelve members were Crown appointees, and twelve, ex-officio, from the City. The members were unpaid and appointed for two-year periods. Some 200,000 cesspools were abolished. Pipe sewers were connected to all houses fitted with water-closets, and the sewers emptied raw sewage into the Ravensbourne, the Lee, and the Thames.

The rising tide choked many of the sewer outlets, with results that can readily be imagined – the falling tide left behind an appalling jetsam. During slack water, at high tide, the solids in the choked sewers were deposited, and remained behind. Communities outside the Commission's jurisdiction all disposed of their sewage to the Thames.

In 1849 another epidemic of cholera claimed more than 14,000 lives in London alone. The then Commission proposed that the sewage be kept out of the river, and that lines of sewers should empty into sumps, from which it could be pumped out on to agricultural land. Mr Phillips, the Chief Surveyor, again recommended Martin's intercepting sewer scheme, proposing to carry the outfall still further downstream. The Board of Commissioners wavered, and called for alternative competitive schemes, of which 116 plans were received. This caused such confusion that the Board could not even make up its collective mind (sic) and resigned.

Their successors favoured a plan submitted by MacLean and Stileman, who, again using the original Martin idea, proposed to conduct the sewage to the sea. But because Robert Stephenson of railway engine fame was a member of the Board, at the same time they put forward an idea of their own. Mr Forster, Stephenson's able assistant, drew up a scheme. This included an intercepting high-level sewer, into which sewage would be pumped, together with reservoirs at Woolwich Marshes, to hold the sewage until it could be released to the outgoing tide. Steam engines would be used to work the pumps. On the north side of the river the system was more complicated, but again partly involved pumping and intermittent storage, at Gallion's Reach. The scheme was estimated to cost £1½ million, and as the Board had no power to raise the money – nothing was done.

On the new fifth Board of Commissioners was Captain Vetch,R.E. who, in 1852, put forward his own proposal, which again provoked divided counsel. At the same time, Parliament was confronted with Norwood's old plan, plus another for a deodorising manure processing plant, submitted by a private company.

Meanwhile, in 1854, the recently constituted Board of Health proposed separate sewage and stormwater removal, and although the Home Secretary approved, the Consolidated Board of Sewerage did not, and resigned. Sewage continued to empty into the Thames while the Sixth Commission also discussed plans but came to no decision, except that they were 'incompetent to cope with the problem'.

Then cholera struck again, and 11,000 people died. To make matters worse, the stench arising from the mudflats of the Thames in the summer of 1855 became intolerable and the window-blinds of Parliament House facing the river were daily soused with phenolic disinfectant in an effort to combat the stench! Sir Benjamin Hall of Big Ben fame, First Commissioner of Works, whose proposals to deal with the sewage situation were being obstructed in the Commons, suddenly found that resistance had given way. The Metropolitan Management Act was passed, creating a Metropolitan Board of Works, and this centralised authority at last overcame the confusion of local entrenched powers that for so long had hampered the Commission.

Forster's scheme, which incorporated Martin's, was put into effect in 1858, twenty-eight years after Martin, and seven years after Forster. During these last years the removal of filth from the sewers blocked by the tide cost £50,000 annually, and in the summer months £900 per week had been spent on deodorising disinfectants, largely for the benefit of members of Parliament. Not until 1875 were the embankments and other areas finally completed – forty-one years after the artist Martin had proposed the basic idea.

During all those years of confusion, stench, and epidemics of cholera it was slowly realised by some that the cholera 'poison' was in some manner carried by water. Dr John Snow, a general practitioner, was one of the first. He even published a small pamphlet in 1849 entitled 'On the mode of Communication of Cholera', in which he showed that some 'poison' came from the body of cholera patients, and was transmitted to others by the contamination of drinking water by sewage. Applying his theory, he traced the deaths of the cholera victims in the Golden Square district of Bloomsbury to the fact that they had consumed water drawn from the Broad Street pump. This water came from a shallow well contaminated by seepage from the cesspools in the district. Precept was impossible. No-one believed him as the water was so clear. He acted by removing the pump-handle, and the infection abated.

When Robert Koch identified the cholera vibrio in 1885, his discovery was received, as usual, with scepticism. It was several years before his views were accepted even by the medical profession, although Koch was responsible for discoveries of the greatest significance for medicine. Nevertheless realisation that a water-borne 'poison' was involved gave impetus to Public Health measures taken under the new

Public Health Acts.

Edwin Chadwick is the Avatar of the principles of public sanitation. He was born on 20 January 1800. In these early years of the nineteenth century, the Industrial Revolution was exposing the worst insanitary features of a dislocated and swiftly urbanised society. Chadwick became the nation's conscience and sanitary reformer.

He was trained in the law, and admitted to the bar, but, being impecunious, he earned his living by writing for the *Westminster Review*. It is the nature of these essays that is important to us in our attempt to gain some perspective in human ecology. His articles dealt with possible methods of applying scientific knowledge to the business of government.

His articles in the *Review* attracted the attention of Jeremy Bentham who employed him as a literary assistant, and bequeathed him quite a handsome legacy. This enabled Chadwick to act as a free agent, and as a result he accepted a position with the Commission appointed in 1832 to report on the operation of·the Poor Laws, which had become a public scandal. Chadwick became a full member of the Commission in 1834, and was largely instrumental in drafting the report which brought about the necessary Poor Law reform.

Appointed secretary to the Commission that was to administer the New Poor Law, he was frustrated in his attempts to put into effect the very law that he had largely helped to frame, and in 1846 dissension finally led to the disbanding of the Commission.[2] Chadwick's writings in the late 1820s reveal the cause of the controversy. He wanted the law to be administered by trained experts, not by people elected to local government. He considered that the responsibility of the local authority should be that of inspection only.

Nevertheless this was Chadwick's opportunity in another equally important sphere. Together with Dr Southwood-Smith he interested himself in the matter of sanitation and produced his now historical report on the 'Sanitary Condition of the Labouring Population, 1842'. From the date of the establishment of the Royal Commission on Health of Towns in 1842, to which the report gave rise, he was a Commissioner until 1854, when its work was completed. With the passing of the Public Health Acts of 1848, 1875, and the Sanitary Act of 1866, Britain led the world in sanitary legislation. Chadwick continued his voluntary, tireless activity in the public interest until his death in 1889.[3]

I have used the story of London's descent into filth and stench and disease as an example of the human condition under urbanisation. That the city came back to health and cleanliness was largely due to the efforts of Chadwick.

However, the solution of the sewage problem created others no less important. A water-borne sewage system depends upon an ample water supply. The Romans had gone to great trouble and expense to construct their remarkable aqueducts. They also used a water-borne sewage system, and washed away the excrement by pouring a bucketful of water into the latrine. The public was provided with such latrines, which can be seen today at Ostia Antica – a friendly, communal, open semi-circle of six circular holes in a cold marble seat facing the public thoroughfare! Chadwick had hoped to utilise the sewage, rather than to continue to pollute the Thames. Since that river is tidal, and at the same time is a source of drinking water for the city, Chadwick sought to divert the sewage for use on farmland. This was simply the logical extension of the earlier method of disposal of excrement, water being used as the carrier. Chadwick's hopes were dashed by the evidence and opinion of the great contemporary chemist, Justus von Liebig, whom he consulted personally. Liebig emphasised that the dilution of the sewage by water reduced the essential chemical elements of manurial value too extensively for it to be useful as fertiliser. This was only a half-truth, like the second belief, already discussed, that sewage utilisation in agriculture is dangerous.

In 1859 Justus von Liebig was professor of chemistry at Giessen, the leading chemical scientist of the period, and the founder of agricultural and physiological chemistry. He wrote a series of letters on agriculture to King Maximilian of Bavaria, and these as well as his other contributions on the subject of chemistry and agriculture, have exerted an influence up to the present day.[4] John Bennet Lawes,[5] a wealthy landowner at Rothampstead, together with a chemist named Gilbert, subjected Liebig's discoveries to pot-plant and field trials. As a result, they found that phosphate rock could be reduced chemically to a more soluble form, with considerable advantage as to its efficacy as a fertiliser.

Neither von Liebig nor Lawes failed to express favourable, if not eulogistic opinions on the results of the use of animal and human excrement as agricultural fertilisers. However, it was the contemporary prevailing belief that 'manure' was a *food* for plants, and that carbon was derived from the soil. Liebig was at pains to dispel this ancient belief, and to replace it with another – namely, that it was the chemical compounds *only* that were efficacious in plant growth. It should be stated in fairness to Liebig and to Lawes, that soil microbiology was then unknown. It was not until 1888 that Hellriegel and Wilfarth demonstrated the existence of soil bacteria that could draw nitrogen from the air and make it available to plant roots. They did not know, and therefore could not appreciate, the importance to fertility of the microbiology of the soil. Neither could they know that the carbon-dioxide converted by the plant to carbohydrate molecules, would, in the form of decaying plant remains, supply the micro-organisms of the soil with pabulum for their growth, in the complex ecosphere of the soil. In the twentieth century, agricultural scientists with few and notable exceptions have persistently emphasised the importance of soluble chemical fertilisers as the basis of agriculture but these discoveries came too late to help Chadwick.

So Chadwick failed to utilise the water-borne sewage on agricultural land. Had he known it, there are situations where extensive use can be made of the soil for disposing of sewage effectively and profitably. This has been done at Melbourne, Australia for many years. There, the high evaporation rate favours the so-called sewage-farm method of disposal. This particular farm of 26,000 acres of pasture is grazed by 10,000 cattle and 70,000 sheep and up to 3,000 horses. Some 400 men are employed in the scientific management of the flow through the maze of irrigation ditches. This is possible, because the soil is *not* the inert chemical debris of eroding rock, but, on the contrary, a microcosm of millions of micro-organisms. In this sewage farm they do what they have always done on the manured fields of farm and market garden, and what they have been doing in China for forty centuries.

There are however, good indications that some progress is at last being made towards restoring the balance by application of scientific principles which Edwin Chadwick could use only partially because microbiology did not then exist.

At the present time there are extensive sewage disposal plants all over the world. A typical example is the one at West Middlesex works at Morden. Here the purified effluent no longer pollutes the Thames, the activated sludge being pumped thirteen miles to drying beds, from which the partially dried material is collected for application to arable land. Some of this partially dried sludge is further dried to a moisture content of 10 per cent and sold in bags as 'Morganic' fertiliser.

The next ecological step involved the disposal of both sewage and organic town wastes, by composting the one with the other, thus closing the ecological cycle. Mr J.L. Davies, Borough Engineer at Leatherhead, Surrey devised the first continuous garbage composting process. In 1936 the Leatherhead Council provided finance to erect a pilot plant which sorted the rubbish by mechanical means, so that manual work was reduced to the simple removal of bottles, cans, etc., from a moving conveyor belt. The comminuted garbage was mixed with raw sewage sludge in composting tanks, and then removed and stacked in heaps in which the temperature reached 150°F. from fermentation. This temperature effectively destroys all pathogenic organisms and dries the compost, which then takes the form of a sweet-smelling powder which does not soil the hands.

In Dumfriesshire the Shire Council built a new and continuously operating sewage composting plant at the Barony, which handled in

1951 10,000 gallons of crude sludge weekly, and produced a profitable output of 250 tons of compost per annum.[6]

The sale of such composts as fertiliser was, and still is, subject to fertiliser regulations which are based upon the chemical outlook of the Liebig pre-microbial period. The quantity of nitrogen found by chemical analysis of composts is low, but the nitrogen fixing bacteria they contain continuously convert atmospheric nitrogen into much greater quantities of plant-available nitrate than can be purchased in the form of chemicals at the same price. This is a biological *process* which only the user of the compost can evaluate in terms of greater productivity and better quality. The rate of production of the nitrate is more attuned to plant growth than is that of broadcast application of the pure chemical.

Sooner or later all Western civilised communities will be compelled to adopt these principles. There are indeed many large and elaborate garbage composting plants in operation, but few are combined with sewage disposal, which is the ecological essential.

REFERENCES

1. Besant, Sir Walter, *London in the 19th Century*, A. & C. Black, 1909
2. Report Poor Law Commissioners, H.M. Government, 1838
3. Besant, op.cit.
4. Liebig, Justus von, *Letters on Agricultural Chemistry*, Walton and Maberly, 1859
5 Lawes, J.B., *J. Roy. Ag. Soc.*, England, 1847
6. Wylie, J.C., *Fertility from Town Wastes*, Faber, 1956

READINGS

Wylie, J.C., op.cit., also *Wastes of Civilization*, Faber, 1959
Nicol, H., *Microbes and Us*, Pelican Books, 1955

5. TAKEN FOR GRANTED

'Water, water everywhere, nor any drop to drink'

S.T. Coleridge, The lay of the Ancient Mariner

'Water is one of the most important of all chemical substances. It is a major constituent of our bodies, and of the environment in which we live. Its physical properties are strikingly different from those of other substances, in ways that determine the nature of the physical and biological world.'

Linus Pauling, Nobel Laureate, *General Chemistry*, 1970

'... we will have to introduce three new factors into our thinking if we want to understand biological reactions; water structures, the electro-magnetic field, and triplets or some other unusual form of excitation made possible by water structures.'

Szent-Györgyi, Nobel Laureate, *Science*, 1957

The corollary to Edwin Chadwick's Sanitary Revolution was a corresponding demand for large quantites of water. The story of London's water supply is just as complicated and full of frustrations as that of its sewage disposal, because private water supply companies had sprung up like mushrooms, and it was necessary to regulate separately the points from which they obtained their supplies.

In 1877, A Committee of the House of Commons advised public ownership. In 1879, a Bill to that purpose failed to pass owing to the excessive financial demands of the water companies, amounting to £12 million, for the undertakings themselves, and £33 million for proposed annuities to shareholders! In 1880, 1884, 1885 and 1886, successive attempts failed to pass a Bill to acquire the water supply. Finally, in 1892, the London County Council and Corporation were granted the necessary powers.[1]

Meanwhile competition between rival water companies led to the tearing up, and relaying of pipes, as well as to fisticuff battles between rival gangs of workmen, largely engaged in keeping the streets in a state of semi-permanent obstruction. But those were days when the supply of water appeared to be inexhaustible, even if its freedom from sewage contamination might be debatable.

Today we can no longer take this for granted, as was made evident at a conference on water abstraction sponsored by the Royal Society of Arts in October 1971. Mr Felgate for the Confederation of British Industry, stressed the need for economy in water use in financial terms. He calculated that with combined expenditures, capital and current, on water supply, river management, and sewage treatment, the costs will soon be more than £1,000 million. He went on to say: 'No-one I think, can seriously contest the view that something approaching bankruptcy in water supply can only be avoided by a substantial integration of these three functions.'

The British Isles are favoured by a good and reliable annual rainfall, but countries such as the USA have a wide range of climate from the humid east to the dry west. This physiographic fact has brought to light the nearness in time of limits to supply. Thus in the Santa Clara Valley on the west coast, a fertile and highly productive area is threatened with disaster. In 1910 there were in excess of 1,000 artesian bores, lavishly and spontaneously pouring their waters into the irrigation channels, for this is a dry and in summer hot region. Naturally this water came from the distant mountains on which the rain falls, but in the intervening years deforestation and cattle grazing have reduced the 'reservoir' action of the topsoil so that there is rapid run-off as from a roof. This water, which previously sank into the soil, now flows into San Francisco Bay, instead of percolating down into the aquifer from which the bores once spouted water under pressure.[3]

For more than twenty years geologists and engineers have issued their warnings in official reports, yet nothing has been done to protect the water catchment from which is derived the artesian supply. These reports had established already by 1932 that 70 per cent of rain falling on the watershed ran into the sea.

By 1915 most of the artesian bores had ceased to flow, and pumping had been resorted to. From 25,000 acre feet in 1915, the pumps were extracting 134,000 acre feet by 1923. Like the bosun in a leaking ship, the engineers dutifully reported a 5-foot drop in the water-level each year. Suddenly however, the smooth graph of 5 feet per annum was broken by a drop of 31 feet!

Thanks to better and more powerful pumps, water was being lifted from depths of 166 feet, the valley floor itself having sunk 5 feet in 20 years. This subsidence ruined buildings, water-mains and sewers, and costs of restoration mounted to millions of dollars. The engineers and geologists now calculated a permanent loss of underground storage of 500,000 acre feet, that is, water sufficient to cover 500,000 acres to a depth of one foot. The Federal Government Conservation Service proposed a $4 million water-catchment restoration project. The State Government would not co-operate. Farmers spent some $16 million on more powerful pumps and sinking deeper wells. Finally the spectre that the engineers and geologists had endeavoured to exorcise so many

35

years before had suddenly appeared; seawater flowed in and began to complete the destruction. At last the State Government moved.

There is another aspect of this form of water abstraction from underground aquifers. The rivers of the South of England are fed by overflow springs from aquifers in the chalk. Ever since the turn of the nineteenth century, some of these famous streams had begun to deteriorate owing to the combination of sewage effluent and bore-water abstraction; less water, more pollution. Today, with increasing population, the growth of villages into hamlets, and hamlets into towns, mains sewerage is increasingly putting greater pollution stress on the remaining chalk streams.

The magnitude of the sewerage problem in Britain is disclosed by the figures quoted at the Royal Society of Arts Conference, 1971. The Government plans to *increase* expenditure on sewerage purification by some £400-700 million. This, it was stated, is the greatest increase in expenditure on sewage disposal in British history, and it is evident that such additional expenditure requires time. Unless it is accompanied by parallel water conservation works, more rivers will be ruined.

During the discussions, it emerged that the average lavatory flush uses two gallons of water, compared with the five gallons to which citizens of the USA are accustomed. Furthermore it was stated by a Mr Willis of the British Waterworks Association, that they were testing a Swedish flushing device that used only one pint of water! These are certainly straws in the wind. Clearly the day is not far distant when potable water will no longer be wasted on processes which could be conducted either with smaller quantities, or, which could reuse the appropriately treated water.

If sewerage systems are thirsty for water, so are industrial processes. Consider the lavish use of paper products, the newspapers, magazines of all kinds, wrapping paper, cartons, drinking cups, milk containers, paper towels, etc., all 'throw-away' objects. One ton of dry paper pulp requires for its manufacture, anything from 5,000-85,000 gallons of water, depending upon the type of process used.

Other manufacturing processes are equally thirsty. Textiles require 10,000-75,000 gallons for every 1,000 lbs of completed product. Nitrate fertiliser requires per ton 130,000 gallons. Coke does not look as though water would be required in its manufacture, but it requires 3,600 gallons to make one ton. The list can be extended almost indefinitely. The point at issue is not so much the water requirement, but that it is taken for granted, and gross waste of the product in many instances (e.g. wood-pulp products) is an immense charge against Western civilisation. Much paper product is recycled, but it still requires water in the process.

Water resources have been exploited ignorantly and wastefully.

Britain stands in a special historical relationship with water and soil usage. While Europe was in the throes of the Thirty Years and Napoleonic Wars, Britain was making good use of her maritime predominance. This eventually led to the colonising of North America, Australia and New Zealand by people who had farmed for centuries in a mild moist climate enjoying a gentle, reliable rainfall. The countries to which they migrated did not present the settlers with similar conditions. Summers were hot and dry, and heavy rainstorms common, particularly in North America. In Australia the rainfall was unreliable and evaporation rapid. Moreover, traditional farming procedures were undergoing disturbance. At the outset crops flourished and the demand for grain by the industrialised homeland ensured a ready market. This did not favour conservative traditional farming practice. The great empty spaces were always available to move into when soils were depleted of their virginal fertility, and the axe made short work of forest cover.

In America the effect of this ruthless exploitation has been devastating. In Australia, because the average rainfall is much smaller than that of the USA, the results were mostly confined to the soil. Vast areas of once productive wheatland in Australia are no longer capable of producing crops, and the lonely ruins of farmhouses stand in a desolate landscape. The dust-bowl of central USA is celebrated, and to travel over the once rich tobacco country of the first English colonies of Virginia and Georgia, is to witness a loss of topsoil that needs no special demonstration. Soil erosion cannot be dealt with here, but there is in the USA another aspect of it which is less evident, namely run-off from denuded and impacted watersheds.

Heavy rain falling on a forested slope, or one covered with a thick grass sward, is retained largely, if not entirely, where it falls by the spongy root and humus-rich topsoil. From this it slowly percolates into the subsoil, forming the supply of artesian basins and of lesser aquifers, which feed springs, streams and finally rivers.

When the watersheds are deforested, or the natural grass cover is so heavily grazed as to reduce the capacity of the soil to hold the rainfall, the water simply runs off the surface and gathers into streams, creating eroded gullies in its impetuous rush to reach the lower levels. There, it deposits the burden of eroded soil, and ultimately, on the grand scale, causes the silting of river beds. After heavy rain the river beds can no longer contain the flow and flood vast areas.[2]

This is an apparently childish lesson in the sequence of events and would seem childish indeed were the consequences less grave, and the lesson ultimately learned. But, hand in hand with vast engineering schemes to control what only ecological restoration can remedy, the same destruction of watersheds is permitted to continue.

Now and then we read of some calamitous loss of life and property in some part of the USA due to flash floods causing a dam to burst, and like all such news, it falls on ears so numbed with disastrous wars, and the destruction of life, that we pay only passing attention.

Nevertheless, these American calamities affect us all. The USA is a great food-producing country, and it has long been living on soil and water capital, so that the real cost of the produce is not reflected in the price. When the full cost does finally enter into the price of grains, the world will have to pay. Consider some aspects of this cost in terms of water control in that country, as long ago as 1948. The Corps of Engineers, which is responsible for works of flood control and water conservation, estimated some of the cost as far back as 1900. From that date to 1948 the Federal Government had spent $4·8 billion on flood control projects which were so devised as to provide both hydro-electric power and water for irrigation. According to authoritative statement, the Corps of Engineers had begun to build levees to control the Mississippi a century before, and, by extrapolation the cost in 1948 values would be around $10 billion ($100 billion today). In 1948 the Corps of Engineers estimated that the execution of plans for the ensuing fifty years would cost some $48 billion at the then value of money. Together with the $4·8 billion mentioned above, this comes to $57·5 billion in all, and this represents construction costs alone.

Enormous sums are spent annually in the operation and maintenance of dams, reservoirs, locks, and channels, and there is ample evidence that more than $18 billion will be required merely to repair damaged watersheds. Watersheds deprived of their natural cover of vegetation are chiefly responsible for the silt that is fed into main rivers from their feeder tributaries. It is estimated that the useful life of at least 6,000 of the larger reservoirs in the USA will not exceed 100 years, and a mere half dozen will serve more than two centuries![3]

The dollar costs quoted are perhaps the least of the expense when it is considered that reservoirs drown some of the richest farmland in the country. In their creation thousands of homes have been vacated, and tens of thousands of people displaced.

By June 1946 the Great Tennessee Valley River Control and Power Project had removed 13,449 families leaving a further 1,000 to be evacuated. This represents a total of 70,000 persons. In his book, Donald Davidson writes: 'The majority of the willing folk were the young folk who still had their destiny in the making. The worst tragedy of the removal was in the fate of the older folk . . . for many of these death was hastened by the removal.' According to the Missouri Farmers' Association, the Army's projected reservoirs in the valley of the Missouri River would inundate 900,000 acres of fertile land with a recorded productivity amounting to $18 million annually, that is more than twice the estimated annual loss from floods in that zone. These major floods have been greatly exacerbated by destruction of forest cover on the surrounding watersheds.

When it is realised that these consequences of denuding the watersheds were forecast as long ago as 1863, the feeling of inevitability of human disaster becomes oppressive. In that year George P. Marsh, a travelled and astute observer of the situation in Europe, Asia and Africa, wrote a book entitled *Man and Nature,* in which he tried to warn his fellow countrymen of the fate that awaited their descendants if they denuded the watersheds.

Marsh, who was President Lincoln's First U.S. Minister to the resurgent all-Italy government of 1861, had learned the history of the destructive flooding of the River Arno. The first major flood in the twelfth century destroyed the Ponte Vecchio. In 1333, all the bridges except the reconstructed Vecchio were destroyed, and even the walls of Florence collapsed. The flood reached within twelve inches of the 1966 level, and 300 persons lost their lives.

The hills of Tuscany in Etruscan times were densely forested, and the Arno ran clear the whole year round. The growth of the city led to greater demands for timber, particularly in Christian times, and to grazing of the hills by goats and by sheep, the latter for the Florentine and wool trade. Eventually the denuded, sunbaked hills no longer retained moisture and the Arno dried up during the long hot summers, but deluged the town with mud from the eroded hills during floods. Records show that a minor flood occurred every twenty-four years, and that a major disaster occurred roughly every century. After the 1333 disaster, a certain Vico del Cilento recommended reafforestation of the hills. The city government of Florence however, demurred.

These same bare hills, their slopes scarred by landslides, still preside over the fate of Florence. The mathematics of probability do not exclude a repetition of the 1966 disaster at any time.

However, flooding is not the only possible result. Below the great Hoover dam on the Colorado River, the scouring action caused by water passing through the control sluices has lowered the river channel for eighty-eight miles along its course. The debris thus produced is being deposited some forty miles further down the river, with the result that flooding and swamp formation take place. This effect is enhanced by the silt delivered from tributaries below the dam, because the floods which the dam controls no longer scour the river bed. Above the dam the situation is reversed. The backing-up of the reservoir water slows the incoming tributaries, as well as the main stream. This in turn causes the deposition of sand and silt upstream, with further swamp formation extending for great distances. Thus a complete change in the hydrology and ecology is brought about, and one for which watershed control is the only natural and effective preventive measure. The U.S. Reclamation Service has estimated the loss of water from evaporation from these upstream and downstream swamps to exceed 10 per cent per year in those examples studied.[5]

Silting up of the lower reaches of navigable rivers is a commonplace, and in Australia one of the flagrant examples of deforestation and overgrazing is to be seen in the Hunter River valley of New South Wales, where once deep-sea sailing ships could berth at Maitland, some twenty miles or more upstream. The River is no longer navigable, and is subject to extensive flooding.

It seems that instead of dealing with the ecological problem of degraded water catchments, or the gross waste of a natural resource, we are resorting to desalination by means of nuclear reactors. The cost of such desalination processes is not only very great, but the ecological damage from heating the adjacent coastal water of the fish-rich continental shelf, and the radioactive pollution from such necessarily vast and ambitious schemes, is quite unpredictable.

This subject of watershed control is so vital to mankind, and it provides such dramatic examples of ecological destruction, that this chapter can be concluded with the U.S. official account of the destruction of Farmington in the State of Utah in 1923.

On 24 July 1847, the Mormons established the first irrigation enterprise in Utah. Water from the streams issuing from the Wasatch Mountains was used for the purpose, and fertile orchards and fields, towns and cities, developed as a consequence. But the upland terrain was also used for cattle grazing.

Regularly twice a year, once following the melting snows, and again following summer cloudbursts on the mountains, these streams would swell and occasionally flood, but never gave any cause for alarm. Two of the earliest Mormon settlements were Farmington and Centreville, on the eastern shore of the Great Salt Lake. The irrigated land between these settlements brought prosperity to everyone. The watershed of these streams supplying the irrigation, covered some twenty-five square miles of mountain pasture.

On 13 August 1923, seventy-six years after the establishment of these settlements, a cloudburst fell on the mountains and five of the creeks poured an avalanche of mud, gravel, stones and torn-up trees down the canyons leading to Farmington. The result was havoc. Houses, orchards, roads, railway and irrigation works were smashed and buried in places under six feet of debris. Six people perished.

Every summer thereafter there were minor floods until 1930, when mud poured out again, destroying all the valuable property that had been restored since 1923. This time financial ruin resulted.

The two bad floods caused losses amounting to $1 million in

Farmington, and the resulting public reaction led to an enquiry by a commission of experts. The commission found that the cloudbursts were no more violent than the usual storms that had occurred during the past seventy-five years, but that 'the great bulk of the flood originated on areas near the mountain top where the plant and litter cover had been destroyed or reduced and the soil compacted.' This was due to heavy grazing by livestock, and the burning of stubble to clear the ground for the new season's growth. The resulting mud and stone avalanche of 1923, and the smaller but just as damaging mudflow of 1930, had been due to the scouring of the centuries-old collection of debris from the canyons down which the flooded torrents had cascaded.

Not far away was a basin fed by the Centreville Creek, which had continued to run clear and controlled as usual throughout the period 1923-30. Centreville itself, at the mouth of its canyon, was unscathed. Correctly interpreting the cause of the tendency of Centreville Creek to rise during summer storms, the 600 villagers purchased or leased the grazing uplands, and prevented grazing until the plant cover was restored, thereafter strictly controlling the grazing on the uplands. The plant cover controlled the stormwater, Centreville Creek merely rose to its usual two-foot flood level during the 1923 and 1930 rains, but ran crystal clear between its banks.

Other communities in Utah have suffered from mud and rock avalanches due to the same cause, but the owners of the livestock that caused the damage have suffered no loss! The tale of Farmington and Centreville has all the significance of a biblical parable.[6]

Before leaving the subject of water in its potable capacity and apart from a discussion of methods of purification of sewage effluents, which almost invariably gain access to it, we shall consider the treatment of water with chlorine gas to destroy the organisms of infectious disease.

There was a time not long since when it was customary for the traveller in foreign parts to enquire, 'Is the water safe to drink?' Even if he is a stay-at-home USA or UK citizen today, he may well ask that question, for the water that flows from the tap may have already passed through the bodies of several of his fellow men. The safety of a water supply, from a purely bacteriological point of view, requires continuous high-quality supervision, which increasing population makes vitally important. However, this cannot be taken for granted.

And yet the U.S. Public Health Service, who, from time to time issue lists of cities where Federal Government checks have revealed less than satisfactory local surveillance, reported in the late 1960s that the water supplies of some sixty American cities were either bacteriologically unsatisfactory or a potential hazard to health![7] In too many countries, the purity of water is maintained only by chlorination, despite the fact that the occasional outbreaks of infectious hepatitis, a viral disease,

41

have raised doubts about the effectiveness, *under all conditions* of chlorination of water supplies. Some observers have attributed this failure of chlorination to variations in the content of organic matter in the supply, and they consider that this organic matter in some way protects the virus from the oxidising action of chlorine. The production of mutant types of viruses by chemical means has been studied and reported in scientific journals for more than a decade. Some of these mutagenic compounds contain chlorine, and they may well be formed by interaction of chlorine and organic compounds in sewage polluted water.

The action of chlorination as a bacterial destroyer is purely chemical. The gas combines with water to produce an unstable compound, which breaks up into hydrochloric acid and free oxygen. The acid combines with alkalis present in the water and becomes harmless, whilst the oxygen at the moment of liberation is an extremely potent destroyer of living organisms. It is not the chlorine that kills the organisms, but the nascent oxygen which it liberates.

Recently, Joshua Lederberg, the well-known molecular geneticist, has joined with other prominent investigators in this latest field of biological research in calling for caution in the use of chemical mutagenic agents. He is reported as saying: 'Many geneticists have raised cautions about the chemicals that may cause mutations, and I join them by adding chlorine to the lengthy list that cries out for close scrutiny.' (*Washington Post*, 1969).

The extensive pollution of water supplies by nitrates in the run-off from agricultural land heavily treated with artificial fertilisers can add a further mutagenic hazard. This is because certain bacteria in sewage can convert nitrates into nitrites, and these latter act as virus mutagens under certain conditions.[8]

Nitrates in drinking water are a chemical hazard in their own right. The same certain bacteria in the intestinal canal can convert them into nitrites, which, after reaching the blood, destroy the oxygen carrying capacity of the haemoglobin in the red corpuscles. Infants whose foods happen to be made up with such water have been found to suffer very badly, and even to die of asphyxia. The water supply of some US cities has been seriously polluted with nitrates. It should be mentioned that even farm animals have been killed by drinking such water.

Soluble fluoride, now added to water supplies as a result of high-pressure agitation by the dental profession, belongs to the same group of viral mutagens as bromine and chlorine.

South Australia has a long hot and dry summer, the annual average evaporation rate exceeding the rain precipitation rate. If these facts were reversed, the rainfall would carry soluble salts, including fluoride, into the subsoil. Climatic conditions being as they are however, only the lavish use of piped water maintains the oasis of green parks, lovely gardens and rich vegetable farms, as well as the great areas of irrigated lucerne and fodder crops for the intensive feeding of stock and dairy herds.

Because this water supply is fluoridated, as well as chlorinated, both fluorides and chlorides must tend to remain and concentrate in the topsoil, for reasons given above. However slowly this concentration may occur, the day must arrive when the effect of fluoride, which is highly toxic to plant and animal life, must manifest itself.

Recalling the fact that as a toxic substance ascends the food chain it becomes more concentrated, it is not at all unlikely that farm animals intensively fed on lucerne from irrigated crops will ultimately show signs of fluorosis, before the lucerne itself gives any indication of toxic effect.

I have said enough to indicate that the water supply which is a vital element in the ecosphere, and particularly in the ecosystem to which man belongs, is under grave threat, and in a manner according to molecular biology, which is least expected. The water supply certainly cannot be taken for granted.

REFERENCES

1. Besant, Sir Walter, *London in the 19th Century*, A. & C. Black, 1909.
2. Frank, B., and Netboy A., *Water, Land and People*, Knopf, 1950.
3. ibid.
4. Davidson, D., *The Tennessee from Civil War to T.V.A.*, Rhinehart, 1945.
5. Leopold, L.V., Wolman, M.G., and Miller, J.P., *Fluvial Processes in Geomorphology*, Freeman, 1960.
6. Farmington: U.S. Dept. Ag. Misc. Pub. No. 639, 1947.
7. Report on U.S. Water Supplies, Proc. Am. Soc. Civil Eng., 1943.
8. Stent, G., *Molecular Genetics*, Freeman, 1971.

6. INDUSTRIAL MAN

'The immediate future which is our own desire, we seek; in achieving
it we become different; becoming different we desire something new,
so there is no staleness except when development itself has stopped.
Moreover, development, even in the most refined stages, will always
be a very critical process; the dangers to the whole structure of
humanity and its successors will not decrease as their wisdom
increases, because, knowing more and wanting more they will dare
more, and in daring will risk their own destruction. But this daring,
this experimentation is really the essential quality of life.'

J.D. Bernal, F.R.S., *The World, the Flesh and the Devil*, 1969

When did it all begin – the pollution, the disturbance of the ecosphere?
When did we begin to see the solution of mankind's problems in terms
of economics. Having broken the life-maintaining cycles in the ecosphere, why do we look solely to mechanical means to mend the break,
pouring fertilisers on the ground. How have we become so reliant on
that sort of solution? We will examine this kind of question in the next
two chapters.

All the basic technology which is the root of our Western civilisation
is not some new thing, suddenly arisen to destroy us in its accelerating
effect on our environment. European civilisation has for many centuries
been acquainted with land surveying, mining operations, the pumping
of water, and the use of water and wind power, with the exception of
the power to drive this technology and this depended upon the
discovery of new sources of energy. Even associated forms of 'pollution'
had been experienced long ago. Mining has always created heaps of
rubble and slag. Etruscan slag heaps near Populonia are being reworked
today. Drainage from these heaps must have poisoned streams and the
smelting of ores must have distributed arsenic, copper and lead fumes
over the surrounding area. In fact, some believe chronic lead poisoning
to have been a contributory factor in the fall of Rome. The ruling
classes, especially, used, as already noted, vessels of lead to contain
wine, and their water supply was carried by lead pipes. Even the crafts-
men who worked the lead must have suffered. By the sixteenth century
after the turbulent centuries that followed the disruption of the Roman
empire, all this technology had become the firm basis of a flourishing
and sophisticated economy. Equally, by that time, all the methods of
commerce and finance had been laid down in principle, if not in detail,

as they exist today.

The science of political economy dates from 1776 with the publication of Adam Smith's *Enquiry into the Nature and Causes of the Wealth of Nations*. He concluded that, provided individuals were left unhindered in the pursuit of their own interest, *but within the bounds of common decency and the rule of law,* the body politic and its component individuals would enjoy the greatest wealth and wellbeing. Government interference with this process, he concluded, could only restrict the production of wealth.

Smith considered, reasonably enough, that human beings were propelled and guided by self-interest. This has been called 'enlightened self-interest', for in practice he believed it would not assist a man to his goal if he antagonised others. Smith was a philosopher, and although he realised that 'the wretched spirit of greed and monopoly was abroad' he still had faith that self-interest favoured the accumulation of wealth by a nation. He also clearly perceived that division of labour would increase production, and foretold in effect, modern mass production. Through all this ran the theme that wealth would ultimately be distributed through the whole community.

Within less than fifty years, David Ricardo, no philosopher, but a brilliantly successful broker, wrote his *Principles of Political Economy and Taxation*. He did not share Smith's optimism, and contended that the natural course of events would keep labour at the subsistence level. Moreover, he believed that the continued increase in population would compound this evil. In other words, Adam Smith's best of all possible worlds was for him a poor thing. Ricardo's *Labour Theory of Value,* which takes us back to Aristotle, plays an important part in modern economic analysis.

Another important fact established by Ricardo is that each additional increment of work or expenditure on producing food from the soil, tends to produce a diminishing increment of returns. We shall see in connection with the ecological approach, how important this observation is. Moreover, when we examine the social impact of the introduction of the potato by Sir Walter Raleigh, we shall appreciate the truth of Ricardo's theory of the subsistence wage.

Economic activities and their associated phenomena of credit, interest charges, and so on, have been part of the life of Western civilised man for a long time, but our knowledge of the historical aspect is quite recent, and the logical study of these activities is not much older. In fact, David Ricardo the broker and Thomas Malthus the clergyman-economist were contemporaries (1772-1823).

The introduction of the potato occurred at the moment when industrialising England needed the cheapest possible labour. Perhaps the upsurge of industry due to capital investment may never have

45

occurred, at least in that form, but for the availability of this odd-looking tuber. Certainly it proved the correctness of Ricardo's opinion on wages.

There is no greater contribution to our knowledge of the part played by a foodstuff in relation to modern economic history than that made in 1949 by Redcliffe Salaman, in his monumental *History and Social Influence of the Potato*. Although his major interest was virus research (he was Director of the Potato Virus Research Station, Cambridge), he was led of necessity into examining the cause of the Irish potato famine, and the changes that had taken place in agriculture in Great Britain and Ireland during the sixteenth, seventeenth and eighteenth centuries.

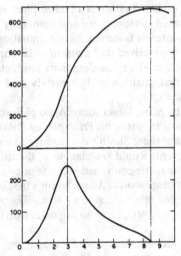

Fig 9. *Ricardo's Law of Diminishing Returns.*
The upper curve plots units of agricultural production per annum against units of labour or power or fertiliser used in production. The lower curve which is derived from it, expresses units of production for each unit of labour etc. The vertical lines intersect the curves where further increments of labour etc. begin to produce smaller increments of output, and also where a negative response results. After the first point is passed, costs of production and price of product rise with increasing disproportion. This point has been passed in many instances in the U.S.A. and U.K.

The pre-Colombian adventures of the potato, as described by Salaman, are fascinating in themselves, but the European phase of them is devastating in its relation to the economics of the seventeenth century.

Whether the potato reached Ireland from a wrecked Armada galleon or through the offices of Walter Raleigh may never be precisely

46

determined. However, it was already growing in Ireland between 1566 and 1588. William Cobbett, that patriot of vision and discernment, wrote at the beginning of the nineteenth century: 'It was the greatest villain upon earth, who they say, first brought the root to England.'

At this period, trade between nations had escaped from the moral strictures of the Church, and was being enthusiastically conducted under the following general principles:

1. The importance to a nation of a good stock of gold or silver.
2. The greater importance of foreign over domestic trade.
3. The greater importance of manufacturing over production of raw materials.
4. Intervention of the State to achieve these objects, and the value of a large population as an aspect of national greatness.

The potato provides the most valuable and plentiful food crop that can be grown. It contains 2 per cent protein of high nutritional value, 19 per cent carbohydrate, a surprisingly high content of vitamin C and an appreciable quantity of Vitamin B complex, as well as minerals. All these add up to good nutrition when potatoes become the staple article of food. Together with parsnips and milk this diet, as it did in Ireland, becomes more than adequate. It was almost the secret weapon of Germany in World War I. In Ireland, the population, halved by war and repression, not only survived but increased whilst living in penury. Their lives were saved by the potato.

The outcrops of coal on which was built industrial England followed the line of the New Red Sandstone geological formation. This is marked almost precisely by the Rivers Trent, Avon and Severn. Salaman, searching with scientific precision the relevant literature and reports of the period, quite convincingly showed that the region to the west and north of this line is rich in coal, iron and water, and there industries migrated or were established with the onset of the Industrial Revolution. Here also another migrant appeared in plenty – the potato.

William Cobbett,[2] considered that the potato had reduced the Irish peasant to a state of slavery, and called it 'Ireland's lazy root' – mistaking cause for effect – or 'the root of extreme unction' – which was nearer the mark. He suspected economic oppression whenever he discovered a family using the potato as the chief ingredient of a meal. He found, for example, that in the west country the potato was used instead of bread. Moreover, he had learned from Agricultural Committees that it was customary to allot the labourer a potato patch in part payment of wages. Already at the beginning of the nineteenth century, Cobbett foresaw the danger which threatened the labourer if he allowed the potato to replace wheat in his family diet. He was certain that such a change would destroy the relation of master and man. He asserted that manual labourers would not, unless compelled by necessity, forsake their well-established diet of meat, milk, cheese and bread, for potatoes. The Iron Law of Wages of Ricardo, however, had its way. The 'labouring poor' were encouraged in the early nineteenth century to raise potatoes for their own subsistence, by developing labourers' allotments as a national economic policy. The avowed object was to wean them away from the more expensive diet based on wheaten bread.

Salaman quotes Thomas Estcourt of Longnewton, Wiltshire,[3] who let allotments on fourteen years lease to labourers on condition that they planted at least a quarter with potatoes and did not accept poor relief. This scheme, Estcourt claimed, adopted by local workers, rescued the parish from misery and ruin. One contemporary 'reformer' of this type records the pious hope that potato allotments would eventually bring about a reduction in wages, lowering of the poor-rates, and the breaking in at an early age of the labourer's children to the routine of farm work.[4]

My purpose in making this incursion into the social influence of the potato has been to illustrate the dire consequences that can result from a climate of opinion concerning the nature of human economic activities.

Let us now look at another example of man's economic approach. In the United States, beef production is currently based on the 'feeding lot' principles. The 'feed' is grain-based, but hormones are used in order to bring about fast weight increases. It is the *rate* of increase that is significant from a commercial point of view. The hormone used is a synthetic female hormone, which increases the rate at which a steer puts on weight by as much as 20 per cent. Animals on a feed lot are reared and fattened like poultry in a battery. They must be carefully watched for any signs of departure from normal health. Like battery poultry, because they are not using their muscles by grazing and selecting their own food plants from a natural pasture, they are in an artificial environment made more so by the implantation of hormones. Unless the hormone dose and the feeding formula are both used with expert care, results may not be good either from an economic or a trade grading point of view.[5]

The increase of weight seems to be due to an increase in protein as well as intra-muscular fat (marbling) provided cautious skill is exercised. With every increase in protein there is a proportionate increase of water content, amounting to four-fifths of the dry-protein weight. Now, whether the grade from a trade point of view is good or excellent, it can be safely asserted that from a taste point of view, the result is dismal. American grain-fed beef compares unfavourably in palatability with the Australian range-fed product.

Let us now look at what might be termed an experimental trial of the economic system that has evolved in Western civilisation. Such an experiment is being made on a grand scale in the 'underdeveloped' countries. Dr Conrad Seitz, a German official in Delhi, presented a paper at a seminar in Tokyo in April 1971 on 'Education to Peace'.[6] The address deals with the fact that development aid is not achieving the aims for which it was intended. The observations of Dr Seitz give a most valuable standpoint from which to look back on the Industrial Revolution in the eighteenth and nineteenth centuries. He believes that the failure of aid to achieve its desired aim is caused by the application of archaic economic theories. Briefly the current theory is that 'advancement' of these countries depends on the development of industries. Development of industries needs capital, and because these underdeveloped nations are poor, the thing to do is to provide the capital. Because the countries providing the capital in the form of loans wish to ensure that the most effective use is made of such capital, their economic and technical experts become responsible for the decisions as to the type of industry to sponsor. Given the initial capital impetus, the industries will, as they get under way, generate more capital out of the savings made from increasing incomes, until finally the system becomes self-sustaining. At this point, there is no need for further aid, and national wealth begins to filter through to all members of the community.

The significant carry-over from the eighteenth-nineteenth centuries is the belief that industry is the essential means to general prosperity, that people engaged in agriculture must move into the factories, and that the small farms be merged into larger holdings. The final stage of agricultural development is that it too shall be converted into an 'industry'.

The application of this theory presupposes heavy withdrawal of savings during the stage of early rapid growth, and this tends to widen the income gap in the interest of future benefit, just as we saw from the history of the potato. Moreover, the object of capital accumulation is more swiftly achieved by capital intensive industries. This of necessity lowers the demand for labour, except among the well-trained and practically skilled groups.

Development aid, pursued along these lines, overlooks the human aspect of the situation, the traditional institutions, and the traditional value judgements of the people themselves. These, unlike our purely material basis of assessment, have been an obstacle in the path of Western innovations. Capital accumulation as a goal distracted attention from the social milieu.

To make matters worse, the rate of increase of population is three times as great as it was in nineteenth-century Europe. This is due to the work of modern medical scientists, who have reduced the morbidity and mortality rates due to endemic diseases such as malaria, yellow fever, kala azar, and sleeping sickness from a hitherto unbelievably high figure.

There are other factors overlooked by the purely economic assessor. In the nineteenth century there was opportunity for migration by dispossessed or unemployed agricultural labour. The USA, Canada, Australia and New Zealand are an aspect of the 'hidden costs' in the simple calculations of economists. There is also the influence of the potato to which we have already referred. In the developing countries, therefore, a land policy that uses the agricultural sector merely as a source of industrial labour is bound to produce a dangerous situation, because the capital intensive industries employ relatively so few workers. The developing countries needed labour-intensive small industries tailored to fit the traditional outlook, as well as land reform based on labour-intensive small holdings. In effect we are witnessing a gross example of ecological mismanagement.

Whilst it is true that medical science has been responsible for the lowered mortality rate, the result has been to increase pressure on the means of subsistence. Malthus, who is derided for his views that population would always press on the limits of food production, has been vindicated by the extent of undernutrition and malnutrition in 'developing' countries. In many instances this is so bad as to undermine the will and the physical capacities of individuals to perform useful work (Seitz). This is a further reason why land reform is essential, even if that alone cannot solve the population problem. The times are surely out of joint when a fixed belief in the industrial panacea for all social ills can ignore the simple facts of food production from a plot of earth by people, not by machines. Land reform is at least one way, if not the only way, to ameliorate rural unemployment.

Why are vast quantities of chemical fertilisers and insecticides being used? Surely to increase the yield of produce per acre of soil, and per man-hour per day? It is the outstanding example of the application to a biological process of the methods of 'time and motion' studies of the mechanical processes of large-scale industry. Large-scale is the operative phrase. The economics of scale are continually being emphasised as reasons for mergers, takeovers, and conglomerate formations in every possible field.

The F.A.O. is responsible for the term 'Green Revolution'. This refers to the introduction of new varieties of crop plants which demand high fertiliser input. European and American fertiliser usage amounts, on average, to 90 lbs per acre. If Green Revolution ideas prevail, and three crops per year of the new varieties are raised, this suggests the use of 270 lbs of fertiliser per acre in certain instances. Consider what this means in financial costs to a land such as Latin America, where 10 lbs per acre were applied in 1962.

Tun Abdul Razak, Prime Minister of Malaysia, has advised against producing a rice surplus in his country.[7] Using high-yield strains, and lavish fertiliser, his country's rice deficit threatens to become a surplus. But, says Tun Razak, 'we cannot export it, because it is the most expensive and poorest quality rice in South East Asia.'

Inherent in purely economic solutions of problems are greater and more rapid onslaught on the ecosphere, by the use of machines and chemicals, together with loss of human contact with the soil, and therefore loss of a conservation outlook.

We have all become accustomed, by gradual degrees for some centuries, to such an outlook, the present situation differing from that of the sixteenth century only in degree and in rate of change.

The words of Cassius, taken from their context it is true, express the situation better than any I could use: 'Men, at some time, are masters of their fates: the fault, dear Brutus, is not in our stars, but in ourselves . . .'

REFERENCES

1. Tawney, R.H., *Religion and the Rise of Capitalism,* Pelican Books, 1937
2. Cobbett, Wm., *Rural Rides,* 1825
3. Salaman, R., *History and Social Influence of the Potato,* Cambridge University Press, 1949
4. Thomas J. Crutchley, Communication to the Board of Agriculture, vol. 1, 1804
5. Cole, H.H., *Livestock Production,* Freeman, 1962
6. Seitz, C., 'Education to Peace', Europa Archiv, 23/1971
7. A radio broadcast on 2 April 1972

READING

Energy and Power, Sci. Am. Pub., Freeman, 1970. A collection of highly significant articles by experts.

7.   SCIENTIFIC MAN

'I believe that we are at the beginning of changes as important as those initiated in the Classical era of Greece, or the new learning of the Elizabethan period. These are concerned with our attitudes and motivation in respect of knowledge and its application. There is a growing belief that people matter more than things.'

Sir James Taylor, Inaugural address Royal Society of Arts, 1972.

Technology is as old as the first lever used by primitive man to move a stone. Through the ages, since Archimedes devised his cochlea (screw) pump for raising water, pulleys, levers, toothed wheels, windlasses, horse-driven power mills, water-mills and windmills have been used by man. Yet it was not until the late seventeenth century that experiment became a recognised method of establishing the facts from which theories could be developed.

The Royal Society for the Advancement of Learning received its Charter in 1662, but it was not until 1800 that the Royal Institution was established to educate and create general interest in the mechanical arts. The Royal Society for the Encouragement of the Arts, Manufacturers and Commerce was established in 1745.

The inventions by Arkwright of the water-frame to produce yarn for warping in 1769, and by Crompton of the spinning mule ten years later, and the power loom by Cartwright in 1785, were all driven by water-power. These had already led to the mechanisation of spinning and weaving and of factory production of cloth, before the application of James Watt's steam-engine, which finally sealed the fate of cottage industry. Watt's engine was originally devised to improve on that of Newcomen (1712), which was used only for pumping water from mine shafts. As Watt's engine became improved it was adapted for use in textile factories, and the accelerating changes due to mechanisation were well under way. None of this development, however, depended upon science. It was due to the natural inventiveness of practical man. All of it, for 150 years, was an adaptation to mechanisation of the hand processes long used by artisans.

This was the period when the views of Adam Smith, taken out of the context of 'enlightened self-interest', were used to justify an inhuman attitude to the workman, transformed into a 'factory hand'. The rural crafts of the greater part of England had involved a healthy personal relationship between master and man. The factory altered this. The overseer was charged with getting the most from the workers, while the owners, partners or a joint stock company, were far removed from personal relations with a mass of millhands. This alienation gave rise to the worst aspects of the Industrial Revolution. It is a shock to learn that even William Wilberforce, whilst relentlessly campaigning against the slave trade, could state that it was incumbent upon the poor 'faithfully to discharge their duties and contentedly to bear their inconveniences.'

The development of scientific logic and experiment had completed the already advanced scepticism about the bases of the beliefs propagated by the Church. A strong undercurrent of materialism was already running by the beginning of the nineteenth century. The first half of that century has rightly been called the Age of Paradox, and it reflects enormous credit on reformers like Ashley and Owen, that the squalorous, stinking living conditions and the factory maltreatment of the working class, were eventually rectified by Act of Parliament.

The influence of science on the social history of man has been brief, but momentous. From the discoveries of Ohm, Oersted, Ampere and Faraday, relating to magnetic phenomena, came practical developments of great significance: of the electric telegraph, telephone, electric motor, dynamo, and electric light. J.P. Joule's establishment of the quantitive relation between heat and work, namely the Mechanical Equivalent of Heat meant that steam power from that time onwards could be measured, just as one could measure electrical power, and since the one produced the other, energy costs of production could be calculated. Faraday published the account of his magneto-electric machine in the *Philosophic Magazine* in 1822, and after many developments of his discovery, Siemens in 1867 presented to the world the first dynamo-electric machine, that is one which created its own magnetic field and did not rely on 'permanent' magnets, and by 1893 electric motors were being used for all purposes including traction. However, the real impetus to power transmission, which in the form of direct current electricity is somewhat restricted, was given by the practical develop-ment by C.E. Brown of Tesla's idea for using alternating current. The motor was built by the Oerlikon works, Switzerland, and shown at the Frankfurt Exhibition in 1893. Thus did polyphase alternating current begin to revolutionise power transmission.

The development of power and light distribution has taken place during the last eighty years. To this, the Curies, Rutherford, Bohr and Einstein added their twentieth century cataclysmic ideas on the nature of matter and energy.

As with electricity and heat, so with chemistry; the same period illustrates the advances made as soon as accurate measurement was applied to observed phenomena. Following the earlier work of Boyle,

Mayow and Black, Lavoisier laid the cornerstone of quantitative chemistry in 1772. Then, Priestley's discovery of oxygen in 1774 enabled Lavoisier to define more precisely the changes he had so meticulously measured. Moreover, he was swift to recognise that the same oxygen that combined quantitatively with metals was also the essential substance in animal respiration. Among many other observations, he defined a salt as being a combination of an acid with an oxide. Although greater precision was to come with the discovery of chlorine by Faraday, nevertheless this concept was to prove most fruitful.

When Lavoisier's quantitative methods were applied by others it was soon discovered that, when a substance forms several combinations with another, the weight of one being taken as a constant, the weights of the others vary in simple numerical proportions, i.e. 1:2, 1:3, 2:3, 1:4, etc. This is Dalton's great contribution, the Law of Multiple Proportions. This law (1803) contained the germ of atomic theory, because unless matter were reducible to units of some kind, how could this phenomenon be explained? Many quantitative experiments around this period led to the conclusion that the elements of matter consisted of molecules of identifiable weights.

The ancient Greek philosophers had postulated the existence of elementary particles, but now there was experimental proof. Thus, from the start of the twentieth century began a breath-taking series of discoveries and revelations. In the latter class are the various attempts to arrange the known elements in groups having a 'family resemblance', the so-called atomic weights being listed with them. These weights were determined relative to that of the lightest, hydrogen, and were tantalisingly close to whole numbers, but not quite. Herein lay the germ of further discovery, but when Mendeleev in 1869, and, contemporaneously, Lothar Meyer, arranged the elements in what they termed a 'periodic table' (because of the periodicity of family resemblance), Mendeleev asserted that, where gaps appeared in the table, there were still undiscovered elements. This prophecy led to search, and search led to their discovery.

Quantitative relations were soon revealed between electricity (though its nature was then unknown) and chemical elements — as well as between the heat content and chemical reactions.

Coterminous with these investigations were those made with what were termed organic compounds, namely those formed by plants and animals and hitherto believed due to 'vital processes'. At first this work aimed at isolating in a pure form, and identifying such substances as quinine, strychnine, morphine, but not until Wohler in 1828 artificially prepared urea, a typical organic compound, was the first step taken to dispel the mystery of these processes.

Liebig had already found that two organic substances, silver cyanate and silver fulminate, though identical in composition, had different properties, and Wöhler showed that urea and ammonium cyanate demonstrated the same phenomenon. Here we are at the beginning of structural chemistry, that understanding of chemical interactions which has led to the development of plastics and to an understanding of the alpha-helix of DNA.

Apart from chemicals such as drugs, pesticides, herbicides, and dyestuffs, the chemical industry had produced artificial fibres and sheets from natural cellulose before the 1939-45 War. During that war, however, an artificial fibre called nylon was produced by a chemical process. This was a direct result of chemical discoveries of the structural relationships of the molecules that form silk, wool and rubber, all long chains of molecules of the same kind, called polymers. The same sort of chemistry has produced thermo-plastics of two varieties, one that can be moulded by heating till it softens, the other that sets permanently on mixing the ingredients. We are all now well acquainted with these materials in domestic use.

The chemical industry now depends largely for its raw material upon the petroleum industry. Its high demands, combined with the enormous increase in the use of motor vehicles, creates an ever-greater need for the production of crude petroleum, and promotes the expansion of the ancillary activities such as construction of pipelines for gas and petroleum, mammoth tankers, drilling rigs and prospecting and refining. All of these activities are associated with waste, some of it toxic, the disposal of which is a major problem. These new activities are also associated with an increasing outlay of investment, both directly and indirectly, in the construction of new power stations many of them nuclear. The burgeoning aviation industry, too, raises its own problems, of a mixed mechanical and chemical nature, all of them involving ever-increasing demands for power.[1]

The sciences, whose history we have so cursorily reviewed, deal essentially with simple categories. These can be isolated, metrically studied, and the results subjected to a particular logic in order to establish their right to be considered as related to current scientific belief. The categories of physics and chemistry can be brilliantly manipulated to achieve specific economic ends; ends achieved by a two-way disturbance of the ecosphere. It is exploited to secure raw materials and power; its ecosystems are disrupted by deflecting their natural input, or poisoned by non-degradable contaminants such as detergents, pesticides, and radio-isotopes.

Technology, which is the practical application of scientific information, functions at the behest of industry or government, not in its own right. It is, therefore, quite beside the point to speak of it as Zuckerman has done: 'We must never confuse the present likely course, along which

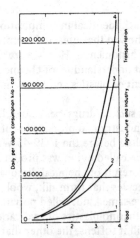

Fig 10. *Energy used by Man at different stages of historical development:*
  1. *Primitive agricultural Man.*
  2. *Advanced agricultural Man who had access to coal for heating.*
  3. *Industrial Man who used wind, water and steam power.*
  4. *Technological Man using electricity and internal combustion engines,
     nuclear power and aviation.*
*Curve 1 shows that there has been little increase in energy purely for food
production, but Curve 2 shows that more energy is being used by the
agricultural population. Curve 3 shows a steep increase owing to the use of
steam power and·fuel heating by the community, while Curve 4 shows an
enormous increase in power usage by the general application of internal
combustion engines for transportation. Both curves 3 and 4 are strongly
influenced by electric power distribution.*

we are driven by technology, as the only necessary course'; or, 'It is
clear that the process (increasing labour productivity) is not conditioned
at its start by any broad conception of what the environment of man's
future should be.'

Cole[2] has stated that the USA consumes 25 per cent of the world's
total power resources. The more power we use, the more we want. The
shape of our cities is moulded by the consumption of energy. It affects
our economic and social pattern, and breeds a certain self-conceit
concerning our urban superiority. Certainly no-one even contemplates
a time when power may not be so readily available.

All new developments utilise more power. The motor vehicle
industry has produced a veritable Moloch in this respect, not only in its
own demands, but in the demand of its products, the engines of which
are designed to produce more horse-power and greater speeds, and
greater rates of obsolescence. Greater compression ratios call for more
anti-knock fuel, and therefore more lead tetra-ethyl. Greater acceleration
rates wear out more tyres more rapidly. Higher speeds call for more
freeways, for which bitumen and concrete demand still more fuel in

construction. The cost of road haulage of goods in the USA according to Commoner,[3] who cites government statistics, is 3,462 British Thermal Units compared with 624 BTUs per ton/mile by rail. The construction of special roads to carry the trucks uses power in the ratio of 3·6:1 in favour of the railroad, which is cheap by comparison, but doesn't pay under existing economic rules.

Aluminium is an example of the replacement of steel, or wood, by a substance that involves much greater demands on power resources. One lb of aluminium requires for its production some 30,000 BTUs of electric energy, whilst the same weight of steel uses only 4,600 BTUs. U.S. statistical reports estimate that the chemical, aluminium, and cement industries use 28 per cent of the total electric energy in that country. To the casual observer, the wasteful expenditure of electrical energy in the USA must signify that the foregoing figure would be much higher if domestic and municipal uses were reduced to rational levels.

Figures, quoted by Cole, show in startling fashion the rapidly accelerated use of energy, particularly that from irreplaceable sources, by man during the past century, from 1875, when the steam-engine came into general use, until 1970. The figures for utilisation of fossil fuel in the USA are equally startling. Recently, Interior Secretary Rogers gave evidence to a Senate Committee chaired by Senator Proxmire. In the course of a long and searching examination into costs, the selection of the Alaska route for an oil pipeline and the Canada route for a gas pipeline from the North slope, Mr Rogers stated that the North slope oil would last for only fifteen years at present rates of consumption. Surely this is a desperate gamble with the perma-frost environment for so short a respite! The following graphs representing the rates of world oil production are taken from Hubbert who was a member of the Committee on Resources and Man of the United States National Academy of Science.

These data are based upon the most accurate information available from oil exploration authorities. Two curves are shown: the most optimistic projection and a less sanguine one. The date at which priorities for the use of liquid fuels will begin to affect individual lives in the affluent western countries is within the lifetime of those born since 1945.

The replacement of natural fibres by man-made fibres in the textile industry has also involved relatively much greater use of power, because the chemical processes involved employ high temperatures and pressures. This industry also makes great demands for electrical power in the production of chlorine, a most important reactant as we have seen. The same industry produces plastics for containers of all kinds, and the non-returnable container is now creating new problems of

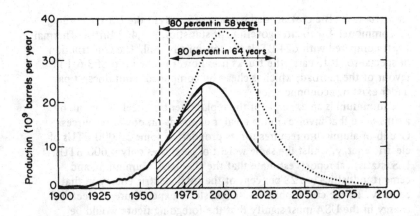

Fig 11. *Two cycles of world oil production based upon different estimates of ultimate recovery (E.U.R.) made by two experts, L. G. Weeks and W.P. Ryman respectively, and quoted in* Resources and Man, *Freeman 1969. The continuous curve is based on Weeks' E.U.R. of 1350 x 10^9 barrels, and the broken curve on Ryman's E.U.R. of 2100 x 10^9 barrels. The dark area represents 182 x 10^9 barrels based on Weeks' estimate, that would be used in the 30 year period from 1960 to 1990. Comparison with the clear area of 184 x 10^9 barrels used between 1900 to 1960 emphasises the enormous increase in the use of petroleum products.*

disposal because it does not burn, nor is it biologically degradable.

Commoner[3] quotes Hanson on the results of a study of energy costs for bottle manufacture, processing, shipping, etc., to deliver equal quantities of fluid; the non-returnable bottle costs seven times more than the returnable! The more one examines these features of our high energy-using society, the more one begins to realise why the cost of living is escalating at such an alarming rate. After the war, the demand for agricultural production was a signal for greater activity in production and marketing of nitrogenous fertiliser. Not only has this reached such proportions as to create a pollution problem of its own, but the widespread use of such fertiliser is, in effect, another form of industrial replacement of soil by chemicals. In the USA the post-war use of nitrogenous fertiliser has increased by a factor of 600, and the yield of corn by the factor of 2·5! Moreover this is showing all the signs of the operation of David Ricardo's Law of Diminishing Returns.

Recently published data relating to fertiliser use and productivity of crops in the United Kingdom have been collected by Allaby and Ottery from Reports of the Ministry of Agriculture, 1971, and

Fertiliser for Maximum Yield by G.W. Cook, 1972. Fertiliser usage for wheat and barley rose from 1945 by a factor of 250 and 260 respectively until 1964, thereafter it falls off. Yield per acre however has remained constant or has fallen slightly. The same is true for oats, potatoes, sugar beet and rye. Total increased production of any crop has been achieved by *increased acreage sown to that crop.*

Allaby and Ottery conclude that animal production, which has continued to rise, is doing so at the cost of imported feeding stuffs. Thus, of 1,983,000 tons of protein concentrate consumed, 1,693,000 tons were imported. This import includes 371,000 tons of fishmeal and 900,000 tons of oil cake and oil meal. Without comment they conclude their report: 'These came mainly from developing countries.' What does not appear in the statistics, is the deterioration of the soil ecosystems, and the effect on overseas agricultural lands, from which animal feeds are produced.

Detergents are commonly compounded with phosphates to improve their efficiency when used with hard water. Although this change is not associated with increased energy demand, it has been responsible for a major and dangerous form of pollution of water supplies, and disturbance of sewage treatment operations. The increase in phosphate in sewage has been found to run parallel with the consumption of synthetic detergents. Moreover, they are not bio-degradable, as is soap; those that are, have been produced in response to government regulation and release phenolic compounds which are both stable and toxic. Their ecological influence is, at the present moment, not thoroughly investigated. Excessive quantities of phosphate escaping into surface waters, lakes and rivers, has led to overgrowth of algae, with a chain reaction of major biological dimensions. This new source of phosphate is additional to the run-off of soluble phosphate from excessive use of phosphatic fertiliser on arable land, together with the increasing discharge of human wastes by increasing urban populations.

I owe a great debt to the report 'Resources and Man' produced by the Committee on that topic established by the United States National Academy of Science. Lord Hinton, referring to this report in his Graham Clark Lecture to the Council of Engineering Institutions, said:

'In the years up to the end of the century we ought to have regard to the warnings of long-term problems that are given in "Resources and Man", but I do not think that we will do so . . . . Posterity makes no contribution to dividends, nor has it any votes in the next election. What other considerations enter into the determination of policy?'

Let us consider one paragraph from the Resources Report touching the future of mineral resources:

'Differences in physical and chemical form of the compounds containing the metals in common rock, moreover, require development of a totally new and complex extractive technology, and the unit costs of labour and capital (and even cheap energy) could be orders of magnitude above those of the present. Such considerations imply that for a very long time to come, metals will come from ores that have metal concentrations well above those in common rock, with only few and quantitatively insignificant exceptions, such as the iron in the magnetic black sands of the Soviet Union.'

In this same report T.S. Lovering refers particularly to the metal mercury, which we have already mentioned in connection with the food chain poisoning noted in Sweden and Japan, and even more recently in Australia. I emphasised the extent of industrial waste of this metal from the Kastner-Kellner alkali process alone.

'The U.S. Bureau of Mines 1965 estimated that the total reserves of mercury in ore in the United States at $200 per flask (in constant dollars) was 140,000 flasks, and that at $1,000 per flask there would be 1,287,000 flasks. The latter is equivalent to current consumption (80,000 flasks) increased at the rate of 3 per cent per year for only 15 years! Even the unsubstantiated logic behind the assumption of a price/grade/tonnage relationship, based not on geology but on past production price relations, does not encourage optimism concerning sources of mercury for the next generation either in the United States or in any other of the industrial countries.

'World reserves of mercury at $200 per flask were estimated by the U.S. Bureau of Mines to be 3,160,000 flasks, but current world production is about 275,000 flasks per year. If the world population were to increase at only half the rate at which the demand is increasing in the United States, far more mercury would have to be mined in the next 20 years than is present in this estimate of world reserves. A price of more than $1,000 per flask might maintain world production of mercury for 50 years or more, but the source of this mercury would be increasingly concentrated in a few large deposits, such as those of Spain and Italy, where cartel action rather than costs per unit output determines the market price. It may well be true that science and technology will continue to provide satisfactory answers to our mineral resources problems far into the future. This can take place, however, only in so far as long-range foresight, lead time, exploration, and research keep pace with diminishing grade, changes in mineralogy, and the need to exploit entirely different types of deposits. It will not happen automatically.'

It is difficult for a scientist to imagine a world without the one liquid metal in existence. It is indeed difficult to imagine how the important fundamental advances in science could have been made had mercury not existed. The common thermometer alone points the question. Perhaps the observations of Lovering have a wider implication because of the critical position of mercury in the scale of industrial materials. It serves rather to startle one into a sense of urgency with respect to man's easy acceptance that some substitute will be found for this or that metal.

Let us now consider some aspects of the latest activity of scientific man, atomic energy production.

In the vicinity of Aschaffenburg near Frankfurt am Main, West Germany, is to be erected one of the largest nuclear power stations in the Western world. There are already nuclear power and steam-power production plants in the vicinity. As long ago as 1959, prior to the erection of a mini-reactor at Kahl in this neighbourhood, the meteorological station at Offenbach issued a strong warning against the project. It was considered unwise to add further steam from the cooling towers to that already produced by two large existing thermal plants in a low-lying region with an annual record of 223 days of smog conditions arising from the high local concentration of industry. On the occasion of that warning, the erection of a 16-megawatt nuclear plant was proposed, and subsequently completed. The present design is for a 2,000 megawatt project.

When operational, this nuclear power station will have unforeseen consequences for the local climate. Its cooling towers are 670 feet high, and will require between 3,250-5,600 million gallons of cooling water daily! One-third of this will evaporate into the already moisture-laden air of the valley of the Main, the rest, at a temperature of 95-98°F., will return to the river. The *Stuttgarter Zeitung* of 21 January 1972 thus describes the result according to the opponents of the project: 'It will convert the Hanau region into a sauna, and be grist to the mill as far as smog is concerned.' The sauna atmosphere would present sufferers from bronchitis and other respiratory conditions with a real hazard and add to the complications of possible influenza epidemics. The smog will not improve the already troublesome navigation conditions resulting from the congested passage of 320 vessels daily.

The Rhine and its great tributary, the Main, are already the subject of national and international controversy on account of their high levels of pollution. The Senkenberg Research Institute in its report on this subject points out that the critical temperature for the already biologically degraded river Main is 76°F. Above this temperature, the Institute claims, all biological life processes will be at risk, and plankton, spawn, fish and plants could die, leaving only the blue-green algae. These would undergo cycles of overgrowth and death with the ultimate result of converting the river into a stinking cesspool.

This monstrous power station is a project of the Rhenisch Westfalische Elektricitats Werke, a public utility. The project has been approved by the Bavarian State Government, despite all warnings and vigorous objection by the people of Hesse across the river. Environmental protection associatons have proliferated and all parliamentary representatives, Federal, State and Municipal, have been under continual pressure to oppose the erection of the plant. The reasons for the opposition are more understandable than even those of the Offenbach Meteorological Station.

In the event of a catastrophe, a nuclear power reactor as large as 2,000 megawatts, would be no respecter of human life over a wide area. In the United States, which leads the world in the number of nuclear power stations operating as public utilities, there has been no attempt to design and to construct a reactor of such a gigantic size. An official statement of the Atomic Energy Commission (AEC) runs: 'Our experience with reactors is limited, and we have none at all as far as large reactors are concerned.' In the opinion of the AEC the Grosswelzheim Project must be viewed as a daring experiment, for the safety of which scientists can bear no responsibility. This obviously relates to the known experience of technologists and designers, that mere increase in scale of construction introduces unknown hazards. As it is, the AEC insists that atomic reactors be located in sparsely scattered areas, and no closer to each other than forty miles.

The operation of nuclear power reactors is associated with hazards to life that are fundamental to their design and construction in addition to those of human fallibility. There is a formidable list of informed authority, including Albert Einstein, Robert Robinson, Edward Teller and Hannes Alfven, all of whom uttered grave warnings of dangers inherent in their operation. Even the U.S. Atomic Energy Commission has recorded that infant mortality and the incidence of miscarriages and cancer are all significantly increased within a radius of eight miles.

To date, it has proved impossible to construct a perfectly impermeable shield around a reactor. According to the report in the *Stuttgarter Zeitung,* the 237-megawatt reactor at Grundremmingen for example pours from its chimney into the atmosphere some 8,640 curies of radioactive elements, presumably in a year although the writer does not state the time period. The Atomic Energy Commission of the USA is quoted as stating: 'Tritium and Krypton 85 are going to be a major problem.' Of all the some 200 radioactive elements released in the fission of uranium in a nuclear reactor, these two are the most dangerous because they escape through all protective shields so far devised for such reactors. Because one-thousandth of a curie is lethal for humans, it would appear that there is little lead-time in which to solve the problem. Already 60 per cent of the ecologically tolerable limit will have been reached by 1980.

It is claimed that a 1,000-megawatt reactor will produce as residue from 'burning' uranium, more radioactive strontium, caesium, and iodine, than have all nuclear bomb tests so far put together. The radio-activity of this 'ash' amounts to several billion curies. This is a frightening quantity when compared with the 400,000 curies of radioactive fissile products of the Hiroshima bomb. The radioactive waste resulting from the production of 1 kilowatt of nuclear power is sufficient to kill 2,000,000 people.

The opponents of the Aschaffenburg project ask: 'What will happen if an aeroplane crashes into the plant?' It lies directly below the main approach path to the great Frankfurt airport, one of the busiest in the world. In any case, what will happen, if because of the scale of size and unknown factors involved, the reactor should 'leak' fissile material to the surrounding air in excess of the minimum uncontrollable loss mentioned above? Faulty design, or materials, or construction, are all possible contributory causes, as well as human fallibility. After all, after a long period of an apparently trouble-free performance, the United Kingdom had its Windscale accident, and as Sir Frank Fraser Darling commented: 'The north-east wind was providential that day, shall we say?'

An epilogue to the Aschaffenburg story, is the question of the disposal of the lethal radioactive waste; this is at a high temperature for 300 years, and lethal for 20,000. Current procedure with the relatively small amounts of radioactive waste from existing reactors is to enclose it in quartz blocks, and bury it 3,000 feet below ground in disused mineshafts. The scale of the problem with big reactors might make this treatment impossible.

Early in 1971, in the USA, the Committee on Atomic Energy announced the proposal to bury radioactive atomic wastes in salt mines near Lyons, Kansas. The proposals were based on findings of studies made by the Oak Ridge Laboratories of the AEC and Union Carbide Corporation (a constructor of nuclear power reactors) and financed by the Atomic Energy Commission.

By the terms of the proposal, the AEC would spend $3.5 million to acquire 200 acres of exhausted salt mines near Lyons together with a further 800 acres of surrounding salt formation. It was proposed to make trial burials as a demonstration procedure at first, in anticipation of the construction of a $27·5 million National Radiation

Waste Repository at the site (Lewis R. Bull, *Atomic Scientists,* June 1971). It is stated that the need is urgent for the following reasons. Between 1970 and 2000 the AEC forecasts an 80 per cent increase in construction of nuclear power plants. Ten of 149 storage tanks for reactor waste have already leaked near Richland, Washington, where the soil was permeated with 237,400 gallons of high-level active waste! After fifteen years of research, the AEC concluded that salt was the most *economical* encasement for fissile waste. Natural salt, the commission believes, is as good as cement, with the advantage that, at *high temperatures* the salt melts and fills cracks that may exist or develop in the surrounding rock.

The AEC proposes to reduce the radioactive waste to the solid state, melt and mould it into a ceramic matrix, encapsulate it in stainless steel cylinders 10 feet long and 6 inches in diameter, and transport these cylinders over great distances, from the processing plants in the states of New York and Illinois, to Kansas, in the South-West, where they will descend to 'salt rooms' 500-2,000 feet underground! What the radioactive security is during this stage is not mentioned.

Twenty of these cylinders would be stacked in a 'salt room', 30 feet wide and 3,000 feet long, embedded during stacking in tons of loose salt. It is calculated that 20 cylinders would raise the temperature to 200°C. or 390°F., which corresponds approximately to a steam pressure of 200 lbs per sq. inch in a steam boiler. The theory is that, at this temperature, the molten salt will flow and seal all cracks and crevices in the salt and bedded shale constituting the walls of the 'room'.

At a 'Hearing' by the AEC, F.L. Cullen, a director of Oak Ridge, stated that it is anticipated that the roof of the 'room' will subside some two feet, and that the floor will rise about the same amount, and that the walls will 'squeeze' in, so that the maximum movement of the cylindrical containers will be 2 feet up and 6 inches sideways. No relative movement of the salt is expected to occur, and this resealing will take place over a period of 100 years. This is indeed a remarkable claim for accuracy of prediction.

But there is another and quite opposite opinion. The U.S. Department of the Interior, Geological Survey, op.cit., expresses strong reservations about the site. It appears that there are 29 gas and oil prospecting boreholes on the site, of which 26 could be adequately plugged, but there is a less than 2 per cent probability that the remaining 3 could be plugged. These could permit access of water which could prove disastrous.

There are, moreover, unlisted boreholes! The American Salt Company operating within the outer 'buffer' zone of the 800 acres has encountered abandoned drill holes, which they contend are responsible for loss of working water pressure due to leakage into the subsurface near the salt section in that area! These companies 'mine' the salt by pumping water into the salt beds and removing the salt in the form of brine.

The Geological Survey does not believe that this project for National Radiation Waste Repository can *permanently protect the population* from billions of curies emitted during the 50,000-100,000 years required for their ultimate decay. Furthermore, the Geological Survey points out that the AEC calculations are based on rock sections compounded of salt and shale, whereas the real structure is laminated salt and shale. The interaction of subsidence, thermal expansion and heat flow, could be responsible for breaking the seal of overlying rock, thus giving access to surface or subsurface waters.[4] Again, in perspective the exchange between Kansas Representative Joseph Kubitz and two Californian colleagues in Congress is of interest. Kubitz said, 'How ironical it is to be required to make a case against a new kind of pollution, so hazardous and so lethal that all existing pollution seems almost inconsequential.' California representative Craig Hosmer replied: 'I get the impression that we should never have invented the wheel if we had thought about it beforehand.'

Both the Lyons and Aschaffenburg projects show how dangerous are such schemes in the light of available knowledge.

For some months there has been controversy over the extension of Consolidated Edison electric power production at Indian Point on the River Hudson, USA. Now, according to the *New York Times* of 8 October 1972, the AEC has ordered the company to produce a plan within nine months, for a cooling system that will not jeopardise the aquatic life of the Hudson. It must be operational by 1 January 1978. It will add a further $ 97 million to the $ 200 million cost of the nuclear power plants.

Nuclear power plants are twice as inefficient as fossil fuel burners, and therefore demand twice as much water to cool their steam condensers. When all these Indian Point units operate, they will draw 2 million gallons a minute from the Hudson. Moreover, the AEC has estimated that 2-5 million young fish will be destroyed merely by being sucked into the maws of the condensers, while the heated discharge will compound the ecological destruction. Dry cooling towers of course demand much energy to force cooling air through the more complex and costly condenser system. Just what effect the enormous blast of hot air will have on the climatic conditions of the locality is anyone's guess.

During the operation of a nuclear reactor, the greatest hazard is uncontrolled melting of the nuclear core. The AEC has until recently considered that the provision of a duplicate water-cooling system will provide ample safety should one of the systems fail. Unfortunately, simulated tests by the AEC have demonstrated that the emergency cooling system may also fail! Hugh Kendall, a nuclear physicist at the Massachusetts Institute of Technology and a sceptic about safety, considers that the molten mass would cause a violent steam explosion which would rupture the outer container and spread a cloud of radioactivity two miles wide and sixty miles long, causing the death of most of the population within two weeks. Kendall and his colleagues consider the accident remote but possible, and they insist on the improvement of the cooling system before they will support further nuclear power extension even with these smaller American stations.

The American Government pins its hope for more power on the development of the breeder-reactor, which produces more fuel than it consumes. This reactor requires liquid sodium metal as a coolant, a dangerous material that explodes on contact with water, which in turn is the source of steam to generate the power. Moreover plutonium, which it produces, is one of the deadliest substances known. It is the basic ingredient of the hydrogen bomb. But, AEC is devoting $500 million to the development of the breeder-reactor with the date-line of 1980. The fusion reactor, which is the principle of the H-bomb, is posing the question of how to contain a nuclear mass at the temperature of the sun. But in the USA, it is estimated, 30 per cent of present energy use could be saved by better insulation of dwellings and the use of steel instead of aluminium in car manufacture. Why not use woollen underwear?

Before leaving the subject of radioactive pollution, we should consider the opinion expressed by the Committee on Natural Resources and Man (American Academy of Sciences 1959) which states, 'Radioactive gases after removal of *most* of the longer lived isotopes and a period of storage of the rest, are discharged through tall dispersion stacks into the atmosphere.'

Further: 'Most present practices in the disposal of radio-active wastes, *other than high level liquid*, violate the first of the three principles stated above, probably the second also.' What were these three principles? In 1955 a scientific committee consisting of geologists, groundwater hydrologists, mining and petroleum engineers was set up by the National Academy of Science to advise the AEC. This Committee proposed three guiding principles which the 1959 report considers to be still valid. The two to which they specifically refer are:

1. All radioactive materials are biologically injurious. Therefore *all* radioactive wastes should be isolated from the biological environment during their period of harmfulness, which for the long-lived isotopes exceeds 600 years.

2. The rate of generation of radioactive wastes is roughly proportional to the rate of power production from nuclear fission reactors. In the period of its work, the Committee regarded the rate of nuclear power and related radioactive waste production as being on the *very low portion of a steep exponential growth curve*. The Committee therefore reasoned that NO waste disposal practice, even if regarded safe at an initially low level of waste production, should be initiated unless it would still be safe when the rate of waste production becomes orders of magnitude larger.

3. No compromise of safety in the interest of economy of waste disposal should be tolerated.

The Report of the Committee on Resources continues:

'These wastes are not being isolated from the biological environment at present, and it is questionable to what extent the same practices can be continued when the rate of waste production becomes ten or one hundred times larger than it is at present, without causing serious hazard.'

It is not only the disposal of radioactive waste which poses problems. For example, the Rhine acts as a sewer for 40 million people. At Felsenheim in Alsace the French wish to avoid the cost of cooling effluent from a projected reactor before pouring it into the river, and propose shutting down the plant whenever the river temperature rises above 'safe' level. This will involve transferring the power load to Central France, which may adversely influence the Parisian water supply! Then there is the discharge of saline wastes from the potash mines of Alsace – 8 million tons per annum! The Badische Analin und Sodafabrik at Mannheim discharges 2½ million cubic metres of water daily of varying colours which stain the banks, as does the flow from Hoechst at Main. At Leverkusen, Bayer and Co. empty almost 800,000 cubic metres of polluted water daily, and at Duisburg the turbidity is so great that one cannot see through a layer 8 inches deep. At Konstanz one can see through a layer of almost 4 yards thickness!

18,000 vessels ply the river, and their detritus, human and other, goes into the stream. 8,000 tons of petroleum waste is delivered by the river to the North Sea, according to measurements over the past three years. When the river reaches Holland, it is carrying annually 120,000 tons of iron, 1,000 tons of arsenic, 1,500 tons of lead, and 85 tons of mercury. Just consider what the fish of the North Sea have to suffer! The salmon which the Dutch were able to catch sixty years ago – 150,000 tons annually – are almost gone. The survivors taste and smell of carbolic

and are inedible! Housewives, according to *L'Express*, have even
resorted to imported Norwegian mineral water for washing linen that
comes in contact with the skin, in order to avoid chemical irritation!
Because Holland depends on desalination of its reclaimed polders for
intensive agriculture, the Dutch are understandably worried by the
Rhine delivering a daily saline load of more than 35,000 tons, coming
mainly from Alsace.

In 1972, a Dutch press photographer, Wim Hofland, developed a
photographic film in a bucket of Rhine water, and published it in
De Telegraaf, to show the Dutch just what kind of water enters their
water purifiers. Photographic developers are powerful reducing agents,
that is, they absorb oxygen. There is little cause for wonder therefore,
that fish have practically disappeared from the Rhine.

The German and Netherlands Governments are prepared to construct
a 500-acre holding and evaporating basin near Mulhouse for this saline
waste, but success depends on the co-operation of the owners of fields
and a hunting preserve. The polders reclaimed from the sea by such
labour, maintained by great dykes and continuous pumping, are thus
at the mercy of Alsatian property owners!

An appropriate commentary on the post-1946 period of exploitation
of the ecosphere was that made by a distinguished biochemist, Erwin
Chargoff, whose important work helped the discovery of the nature of
the DNA molecule. He said in an address entitled 'The Paradox of
Biochemistry' delivered to the Columbia Forum in 1969, 12.(2):1518:

'Our modern sciences began — one could say — around the beginning
of the seventeenth century. Until that time humanity had been
nestling in the hollow of the hand of God. They knew the How,
because they knew the Why. But then the question "How really?"
began to be asked ever more urgently, and this went on for 300
years. Now the light of knowledge — ever bigger and more
fragmented — has become so strong that the world threatens to fade
before it. We are able not only to register facts of nature, but also to
create new ones. We manipulate nature as if we were stuffing an
Alsation goose. We create new forms of energy; we make new
elements; we kill the crops; we wash the brains. I can hear them in
the dark sharpening their lasers. Soon the hereditary determinants
themselves will begin to be manipulated. I'm afraid the "dark
Satanic mills" of which Blake wrote, will be no less Satanic for being
brightly illuminated.'

REFERENCES

1. *Resources and Man*, U.S. Nat. Acad. Sci., Freeman, 1968
2. Cole, L.C., *Scientific American*, April, 1958
3. Commoner, B., *Chemistry in Britain*, Feb. 1972
4. Preliminary Report on the Radio-active waste disposal site at Lyons, Kansas: State Biological Survey of Kansas, 1970

READINGS

Eddington, Sir Arthur, *Science and the Modern World*, Cambridge University Press, 1932
Merejkowski, Dmitri, *The Forerunner*, Constable, 1926
Schroedinger, E., *Science and the Human Temperament*, Norton, 1935

8. THE FOREST AND THE TREES
A Philosophical Interlude

'The Scientific Reaction from Microscopic Analysis. From the point of view of philosophy of science, the conception associated with Entropy must, I think, be ranked as the great contribution of the nineteenth century. It marked a reaction from the view that everything to which science need pay attention is discovered by a microscopic dissection of objects. It provided an alternative standpoint in which the centre of interest is shifted from the entities reached by the customary analysis (atoms, electric potentials, etc.) to qualities possessed by the system as a whole, which cannot be split up and located — a little bit here, and a little bit there. The artist desires to convey significances which cannot be told by microscopic detail and accordingly he resorts to impressionist painting. Strangely enough the physicist has found the same necessity; but his impressionist scheme is just as much exact science and even more practical in its application than his microscopic scheme.'

Sir Arthur Eddington, F.R.S., *The Nature of the Physical World,*
Gifford Lectures, 1927

For the layman who attempts to comprehend the environmental crisis, the first difficulty encountered (apart from that posed by discordant cries for action), is the real problem of knowing where to seek some enlightenment. He will almost certainly have been brought up to believe that science forms the basis of progress to a healthier, happier society. The Children's Encyclopaedia begins that indoctrination in early youth. Now he reads and hears that science is the culprit in this destruction of his environment.

The methods of science consist of refinements of the physiological sensory method by which we learn to understand the details of the world around us. After all, when in infancy we are confronted by a complicated but coherent tapestry, some elements of which move about, while the rest is a fixed background. Little by little we isolate this object from that, and learn to identify. Thus in the end we can identify the trees that comprise the forest, Then, ultimately, we learn to use words to codify our meaning, and the forest becomes many things to many men.

The botanist sees the trees as species and varieties; the forester as a vast tree domain comprising mature and young, healthy and diseased trees, with animals and pests causing damage, and so on. The lumber merchant sees it as feet of cut timber. The hydrologist sees it as a vital part of a water catchment, while the camper and hiker see it as the simple beauty of nature. There is in fact no end to the human appreciation of such a natural phenomenon as a forest.

The scientific study of a forest digs much deeper, and makes even finer identification, even to the study of mycorrhizal fungi associated with the roots of the trees and the mineral elements of the soil.

When this aspect of knowledge becomes classified and the study of various aspects of it becomes extensive, the whole is categorised as a subject of a curriculum of learning, and becomes further institutionalised in a department of a university. The degrees of specialisation that are possible are infinite. So far has this gone, that not many years ago Lord Adrian, addressing an important scientific gathering, expressed concern that scientists had developed such specialised languages that they were becoming incapable of intercommunication!

Thus the layman, seeking information about ecology, will discover that it is not a department of specialised study, but a vast field of knowledge embracing all the various categories of science. How did this happen? By the elementary steps we all take to comprehend the world around us, as I have said. Neither the scientist, nor the layman, is able to see the forest for the trees!

The forest is in fact a section of the biomass occupying a portion of the ecosphere, and the study of its total living situation is a study in ecology.

This brings us into the heart of a controversy concerning the mode of scientific approach to the solution of biological problems. The method that has proved so effective in the physical sciences – that of analysis – is termed 'reductionism'. The method used in biology where living systems are studied as a whole, has been called 'holism'.

This is unfortunate from the point of view of the general public, which may never know the details, but which inevitably has put before it the simplest physical explanation. This perpetuates the mechanical idea, long since departed from modern physics, that Science, given time, will find a solution to any kind of problem.

The application of scientific principles may find a solution to a complex biological problem, but not necessarily by using presently known techniques. It is the unwarranted degree of confidence that is bred by this dissemination of partial knowledge that is unfortunate.

Our brains contain approximately 10 billion cells, and this means at least 1,000 billion macro-molecules. Paul Weiss put this question to his colleagues at the Alpbach Symposium in 1919:[1]

71

'Could you actually believe that such an astronomic number of elements, shuttled around as we have demonstrated in our cell studies, could ever guarantee to you, your sense of identity and constancy in life, without this constancy being ensured by a super-ordinated principle of integration?'

He went on to state that each nerve cell of the brain has an average of 10,000 connections with the other cells of the brain, and, according to the most recent work, the turnover of molecules as part of the metabolism of these cells, means that the macro-molecules themselves undergo renewal 10,000 times during a lifetime, and that, without altering the identity of the cells of which they form the essential part.

'In short,' continued Weiss, 'every cell of your brain actually harbours and has to deal with approximately 1,000 million macro-molecules during its life.'

Studies of this changing scene reveals the loss of 1,000 cells of our brains daily, reducing during a lifetime the grand total quoted above, to 10 million (10,000,000) and thus severing 10 billion cross-connections! Yet, even in extreme old age, a sense of individuality, memories and behaviour patterns are retained.

All this indicates that the movements of the molecules with which the chemist deals, in the living cells (millions of which go to make an organ), are ordered within systems, arranged in some sort of hierarchy of systemic order. Despite the continuous flux of molecular material, this system maintains its overall integrity.

The life sciences, which include zoology, botany, physiology, micro-biology and their subdivisions such as parasitology, embryology and oncology, deal with *systems*, not simple entities such as those with which the physicist and chemist operate. A notable feature of these systems is their capacity to adjust, within limits, to changes of their environment – always in the direction of survival.

Manifestly, all living creatures are composed ultimately of molecules but a living organism, even the most minute, consists of more than molecules, the 'more' being organisation, and neither static nor simple mechanical organisation at that. Rather is the organisation more akin to a game of football, where although there is a basic structure, the players move freely, taking up different positions as the game proceeds. Each player has a function to perform in relation to members of his own and to the opposite team, within fixed rules. The game has to be watched in order to discover how any of the players function. If a cinematograph film were taken of a game, and only one frame projected on the screen, it would be impossible to determine which side was winning, or even what phase of the game was portrayed. The game could not be reconstructed from the one frame.

This is of course an extremely rough analogy. Those who work at the molecular level in biology have every reason to be proud of their results; so have those who have worked at the level of the living organism. Quite obviously the molecular biologists cannot, working *only* at the molecular level, discover how even a simple amoeba functions as a living, reproducing organism. Equally so, those dealing with organisms, cannot follow the life process without recourse to the techniques of chemistry and physics. There is no single way to study the phenomena of life and form in organisms.

There is a further extension of this complexity which comes under the heading of 'molecular turnover' where material is taken in from its environment and returns to the environment, altered in composition, but nevertheless the same in elementary material. This change is called 'metabolism.'

In 1930 Charles von Hevesy conducted on himself an experiment the results of which had revolutionary significance for our understanding of the manner in which metabolism takes place within the cells of the body. Hitherto we had known what went in and what came out, but not what went on. Hevesy drank some of the recently isolated heavy water, a compound of hydrogen and oxygen just as in ordinary water, except that the hydrogen was a rare isotope, twice as heavy as the normal, average hydrogen molecule. Hevesy noted that whilst the heavy water passed through his body just like ordinary water, it was almost two weeks before it had all appeared in the urine. Where had it been hiding? Hevesy had in fact used a form of water with a luggage label on it, so that it could be identified among the ordinary water molecules. Some of the ordinary water molecules behaved in the same way, but could not be specifically identified.

In 1949 Schoenheimer published the results of the application of this isotope labelling method to the behaviour of essential nutrients in the food.[2] Nutrients are the products of digestion of food which are finally absorbed from the alimentary canal, and utilised in the body cells. Their chemical names are amino-acids, sugars and lipids. When 'tagged' with an isotope label, they could be traced in their strange passage through the body cells. The results were astounding to say the least. It seems that instead of taking a direct mechanical route to a place where they were utilised, they milled around in 'bits and pieces' in what Schoenheimer termed a metabolic pool, out of which the changing structures within the cell picked up what was required, and into which were dropped what was not of any further use. The fragments of the used material moved out into the blood stream to be removed by the kidneys.

So the cell, which depended on this intake for its very existence, seemed to be analogous to the appearance of a whirlpool in a stream.

Just so long as the stream kept moving, the whirlpool remained! For this whirlpool analogy I am indebted to Lord Northbourne's book.[3]

Described in crude terms, this discovery revealed the cell to be a purely dynamic structure, like a house made of bricks, mortar, timber and metals. From the heaps of building materials surrounding the site the house is constructed, but with this difference: materials from the heaps move into the structure and out again to the heaps; carriers bring fresh materials and add them to the heaps. Other carriers remove from the heaps selected broken-down bits and pieces, so that the house (the cell) and the heaps (metabolic pool) remain the same size, and the design and structure continues as before, but not consisting of the original material. During growth and development more material goes into the building than comes out. During the stage of dissolution, more comes out than goes in. Alas, this is senility. To complete the analogy, the bricks do not necessarily return to the same place in the structure, nor do the nails, screws, joists, etc. Nevertheless, shape and constitution remain integral.

To return for a moment to the original method we all used as infants — learning about the world around us. The objects selected for identification are in the order in which they impress us by appearance or action. So it is with our education, and our news media. The impressive, and spectacular receive attention. The Theory of Evolution, as expounded by Huxley and the contemporary Press, is a good (or bad) example. The fact that countless organisms have not altered their form over the millennia never made the headlines. The more subtle facts known to modern research, that the biochemical and biological systems of all creatures have also remained basically unaltered makes no news.

Under such circumstances, therefore, when we are exposed to the news that DNA has been chemically synthesised, the notion, which is quite false, enters our collection of mechanistic beliefs that life is about to be produced from inanimate matter. No emphasis is made by the 'science' reporter that the DNA was synthesised with the aid of enzymes from a living system. If he did we would realise that the conjurer's white rabbit was in the hat already before he produced it. The feat was remarkable enough, but the 'order' of the molecules to form DNA was already present in the enzyme. The researchers involved were no doubt embarrassed by the form of the publicity.

We are in our day and age unwittingly conditioned to accept a mechanistic explanation of all living phenomena, in spite of the fact that it can be demonstrated in cold, scientific argument that a living system cannot be built up step by step from its molecular basis to produce a system such as that cursorily outlined for the human brain.

If I have made myself clear, the reader will realise how intricate and delicately balanced is this ecosystem of which we form a part. Little wonder therefore, that we regard with incomprehension the revelation that the environment (ecosystem) is gravely jeopardised both by depletion and pollution.

Another microsystem similar to that of the cells of the body is that of the soil, the microcosm of bacteria, fungi, protozoa, plant-root hairs, etc. These form an analogous dynamic system of exchanging energy and material, and so also does the microsystem of the living cells of the plants. It is this complete cycle of change and exchange of matter and energy (different forms of the same thing — whatever the 'thing' may be), that constitutes the biomass. The ecosphere of air, soil and water, is the stage on which the play is presented, and we humans are, or should be, actors playing our proper parts so far as the future continuation of the play is concerned. Our knowledge of the dynamic equilibrium that is embodied in the living cell is based on discoveries barely twenty-five years old. These discoveries received no publicity.

Looking at the trees, do we think at all of the roots and the soil microcosm? Does it ever occur to us that there is a whole world of activity below the soil level of the living plants? There are miles and miles of roots, and the minute root hairs of a single plant number billions. A single wheat plant has actually been demonstrated to put down 44 miles of roots, and a rye plant grown in a container of approximately 2 cubic feet of earth produced 387 miles of roots in 4 months! This corresponds to a growth of some 3 miles of roots per day divided among 13 million roots! The area for absorbing water and nutrients is further increased by the growth of 14 billion root hairs.[4]

Although trees and shrubs grow less rapidly, they too put down a prodigious growth of roots. It is well known to the orchardist that the area of roots corresponds at least to the area covered by the branches. What he is less likely to know is that the roots may penetrate to a depth of 30 feet and can add up to many miles in length.

The rate of growth of the roots, moreover, depends on the supply of at least two vitamins belonging to the B-group, namely thiamin or vitamin B and pyridoxine. These form essential fragments of enzymes responsible for root growth. They are manufactured in the leaves under the influence of sunlight, which carries the protons which, when trapped in the chlorophyll system, delivers the electrons which energise the living cell system. The House that Jack built!

We human beings in turn, derive most of our supply of the same group of vitamins for our own enzyme systems, by the consumption of plant foods, in which whole grain plays a vital part.

The same root systems interact with fungi and bacteria in the soil in a manner that is essential for their growth. It is now known that forest trees cannot flourish without this close living association of certain fungi with their rootlets. This association is symbiotic, the tree drawing specific nutrients from the fungi in exchange for carbohydrates transmitted to them through the rootlets.

For almost a century after this phenomenon was first identified by Frank in 1847, it was still considered to be an infection. Frank's conclusion that the association of plant and fungus was benign, was not firmly established until relatively recently, 1927.[5]

At the present time, this symbiotic association of fungus and plant root, called mycorrhizal, has been shown to obtain for most plants — in fact, it is almost a universal type of association in the soil microcosm.[6]

The nodules so typical of leguminous roots, have been recognised since Roman times as a feature of this group of plants. It was not until 1887 that two German chemists, Willfarth and Hellriegel demonstrated that the nodules were due to infection of the roots by a soil bacterium. This association is once more a symbiotic one. The bacterium receives sources of energy in the form of carbohydrates from the plant. On the other hand, the bacterium obtains its nitrogen, which is essential for the interstices of the soil. This process is termed nitrogen-fixation, meaning that the elementary nitrogen is transformed in the bacterium into soluble nitrate and incorporated with hydrogen which is obtained from water, to form the first stage of production of amino-acids which are the building blocks of the bacterial protoplasm. As the bacteria die, this protein breaks down into soluble nitrate, which is taken up by the root from the nodule, and ascends in the sap to the leaves, where it is once again incorporated in the amino-acids which will ultimately build plant protein.

But even the entry of the bacterium into the rootlets is due to the influence of the rhizosphere, that is, the zone immediately surrounding the rootlets, which excrete substances attracting the rhizobium bacteria. These latter live freely in soil by utilising decomposing vegetable and animal materials as sources of their energy and protein. They do not 'fix' nitrogen at all in this *free* state. Only when they encounter the rhizosphere of a leguminous plant root do they become attracted, and then, by their excretion of infinitesimal quantities of indolacetic acid, they induce kinking in the plant rootlets which seems to be the first stage in the process of bacterial invasion, and formation of the nodule.

Surely this is a most illuminating glimpse of the manifold processes of the LIVING SOIL, on which alone, plant growth can *normally* flourish. The legumes form the basis of efficient protein food production for man. Protein is the limiting factor to the growth of animals and man, and the legume crops of the world, from clover and lucerne to peas and beans of all kinds, represent the major plant source of readily available protein.

Implicit in this brief and fragmentary account of the vast subject of the Living Soil is the warning that present attempts to mechanise and force food production, in accordance with economic instead of biological principles, by relying *exclusively* on artificial fertilisers, pesticides and weedicides, must ultimately result in the destruction of the basis of human life. Of the nature and extent of 'soil mining' by the Romans, we have detailed records. We know also, that this rapacity was due to a profit-based philosophy which had supplanted the survival-based philosophy of a nation rooted in the soil, which its farmers conserved for the simple reason that their very lives depended on their careful husbandry.

I have been at some pains to insert the dates of fundamental scientific discoveries throughout these essays. My object has been to fix firmly in the minds of readers, the extreme brevity of our knowledge of processes the perversion of which is the subject of universal concern today. The brief time lapse is not an excuse for, but is in part an explanation of human folly. We shall return to this theme in a different context, but it must be apparent that any attempt to deal with the background and perspectives of environmental thinking, must inevitably lead to subdivision, and in turn, to overlap and repetition.

REFERENCES

1. Koestler, A., and Smythies, J.R., *Alpbach Symposium: The End of Reductionism*, Hutchinson, 1969
2. Schoenheimer, F., *Dynamic State of the Body Constituents*, Harvard University Press, 1942
3. Northbourne, Lord, *Look to the Land*, J.M. Dent, 1940
4. Bonner, G., and Galston, M., *Plant Physiology*, Freeman, 1939
5. Rayner, M.C., *Problems of Tree Nutrition*, Faber, 1944
6. Janick, L., Shery, W., *et al.*, *Plant Science*, Freeman, 1969. Oosting, N.J., *Plant Communities*, Freeman, 1956

READING

The Molecular Basis of Life, Sci. Am. Readings, Freeman, 1968

9. AGRICULTURAL MAN

'History celebrates the battlefields whereon we meet our death, but scorns to speak of the proud fields whereby we thrive, it knows the names of Kings' bastards, but cannot tell us the origin of wheat. That is the way of human folly.'

Jean Henri Fabre, 1823-1915

In this chapter I will deal with the body's input of nutrient materials. Logically this must involve 'agricultural man' and because of this, emphasis will be laid upon the history of man's knowledge of cereal crops. Manifestly, prior to this phase of human evolution, man was a marauding hunter and food gatherer, and, apart from a midden in his cave, formed during temporary occupation, his wastes were absorbed by the forest or savannah in the same manner as the ejecta of the beast that he hunted. Even during his pastoral nomadic existence, this relationship still remained substantially the same.

But from the moment he settled to an agricultural life, man remained stationary in settlements, at least until compelled to move by climatic circumstance, soil depletion, or attack by his fellow men. History records a multitude of vanished civilisations that have failed for one or other of these reasons.

But 'modern history' in so far as I have been able to discover, makes no special reference to the part played by agriculture. Jean Henri Fabre, the renowned French naturalist of the nineteenth century, bitterly described this universal contempt of the Western civilised world for the fields and the workers who sustain it. I quote his words at the head of this chapter.

It is well to put food production in our perspective. We take it as much for granted as we do the disposal of our excrement by the sewerage system, or our rubbish by the municipal garbage collectors.

Braidwood, who, between 1948-60 conducted several expeditions into the hills of Kurdistan near the bend of the Tigris River, was able to locate and study the archaeology of several agricultural sites dating from about 10,000-8,000 B.C. Some of the sites he and his colleagues concluded, had been only temporarily occupied from time to time, but, at Jarmo, apparently, habitation had been permanent, and many artifacts other than those associated with agriculture and food preparation were unearthed.[1]

For our present purpose, the importance of Jarmo lies in the discovery of the remains of wheat production and wheat milling by the use of stone querns. The grain had first been charred to remove the husk and to make the task of grinding more effective. Moreover, the wheat grains were proved to be identical with those of the wild wheat that still flourishes in the region. Here it seems, was a primitive farming centre comprising, it has been estimated, some 170 individuals. Wheat had been cultivated as the excavated farm implements indicated.

There are other regions, such as Palestine, for which prior claims to agricultural development have been made, but perhaps one should rather take it that evidence is emerging in places as widely separated as the Middle East and the Burma-Thailand border, that about 10-12,000 years ago at least a settled form of cereal production emerged.

Doubtless, the food gathering period had been marked by the use of the seeds of these wild grasses. The Palaeolithic Central Australian aboriginal, among whose tribes I have conducted physiological experiments during the period when they were still in their natural nomadic state, made use of grass seeds, laboriously collected by ants, which had heaped them near the entrance to their underground nests. These heaps the women and children garnered and, when they had accumulated sufficient, they ground the seed between two flat stones to form a coarse meal which they moistened with a little water and moulded into a cake. This they then baked in the hot embers of a fire.

Carbon dating has extended the occupation of Australia by these people to at least 22,000 if not 30,000 years. Until 1942 they had remained nomadic hunters and food gatherers in these inhospitable regions of Central Australia, because they had no beast of burden and no pastoral animal. On the coast, and along the rivers, the aborigines could find fish, but this did not provide adequate support for a settled community life. These remnants of our ancient forebears remain to demonstrate not that they are uncultured, but that their culture is strictly related to their environment.

The important grasses the seeds of which have formed the basis of civilisations are the millets, rice, wheat, barley, oats, maize and rye. Today, the cereal crop accounts for 70 per cent of the cultivated area of the globe. This fact in itself is sufficient evidence of the importance of cereal grains as foodstuffs. It must have been obvious to man in the food gathering stage, as well as to the pastoralists, that these annual grasses, which renewed themselves every spring were useful as foodstuffs. The Australian aboriginal is proof enough of this. It would have been a simple step therefore to try and grow these plants, and subsequently to cultivate them.

The paleolithic Australian aboriginal could never have succeeded in taking this step, because his native grasses did not include varieties as useful as those mentioned above. In any case the climatic conditions and native fauna were unfavourable for fixed settlement. He was compelled to remain a food gatherer.

At the present time, rice, wheat and maize are the chief cereal crops, and are almost evenly divided in importance; rice however being the largest source of cereal food.

Rice has been cultivated in China for 5,000 years, and on the Burma-Thailand border, if recent finds are substantiated, for more than 10,000 years. Primitive Einkorn and Emmer wheats have been traced back some 10,000 years at Jarmo, and were cultivated in Egypt since 5,000 B.C. Leavened bread was made in Egypt in 2,500 B.C. (Hard wheat, i.e. wheat which is hard to crack between millstones, contains 13-16 per cent protein, while 'soft' wheat which is much easier to mill contains 8-10 per cent).

Obviously the hard wheats are more nutritious and make better bread and pasta (macaroni, etc.), which are the basic foods of the Mediterranean peoples. Maize, that interesting newcomer to the Old World brought back by the conquistadors, was, however, cultivated in pre-Colombian America for at least 80,000 years. This has been determined from a study of pollen grains in bore cores taken from the bed of the ancient lake of Mexico City.[2]

Six-rowed barley, 5,000 years old has been found in Egyptian excavations. The origin of oats is obscure, but it may have appeared as a weed in barley crops, and certainly the ancient Greeks looked upon oats as a weed. In the opinion of some experts, the present well-known variety of *Avena sativa*, appeared as a mutant strain somewhere about the beginning of the Christian era. Rye also, seems to have made its lowly entry as a contamination of wheat or barley in the Christian era. Millet, of which there are many varieties, has been traced as a cultivated plant for at least 7,000 years in the Techuacan valley of Mexico.[3] On the other hand, millet has been used in the Old World in several varieties for a similar period.

Barley, nevertheless, was the main cereal of the Middle East, Egypt and Greece in the earliest period, and was cultivated together with wheat in Egypt. It was in Egypt that wheat attained its primacy among the cereal grains. Barley grist had hitherto been mixed with water and the compacted cake then baked to produce the ancient flat bread, just as the Australian aboriginal baked his grass seed cake, and the Hindu today his barley chapatti. When wheaten grist was treated in this manner it formed a more cohesive mass, and it was soon discovered that if this 'dough' was not soon baked, it fermented and increased in size, and developed a spongy texture as well as a delicious flavour. This caused flat bread or unleavened bread, in consequence, to fall out of use in Egypt, but it became a ritual requirement of the Hebrews, who, remembering the Captivity, were taught to look upon the leavening of sour dough as rotten and unclean. Obviously this is a case of a national prejudice using a food as a basic explanation. Only wheat and rye flour can be used to make a satisfactory leavened bread, and the latter therefore conquered the colder eastern regions of Europe.

The potato assisted maize to cross the Andes by supporting the lives of migrants from the Amazon basin as they crossed the alti-plano, and in an analogous manner, wheat (carrying wild rye as a weed contaminant) travelled from Pontus, the Black Sea region, into Russia. There, the wheat did not thrive, but the weed flourished and, with appropriate care, developed into a nutritious and valuable cereal. Within a few centuries, it had advanced across Europe to France, for it was not only a sustaining foodstuff, but it produced a robust and prolific crop, growing vigorously in exhausted wheatfields.

Particularly important was the Egyptian discovery of leavened bread. This was a palatable and refined method of consuming cereals. Previously they had been eaten only as a gruel, or a flat bread. Furthermore, this was the beginning of two technological crafts, the milling and salting of grain, and the preparation and baking of leavened bread. Milling, of course, soon became a commercial means of restrictive intervention between the producer and consumer.[4]

We can now judge by their long histories how important these cereals are to us. From the early time, grain of one sort or another has been the staple food for man, and has formed the basis of the social administration, particularly in Ancient Egypt. In contrast with the general outlook of Western civilisation, wheaten sheaves still adorn most of our metal coins and printed monetary notes, just as they did in the most ancient times.

In Egypt, the Pharaoh owned both the land and the irrigation system. His surveyors were able to compute the harvest from the extent of the area covered by the annual flood. The fellahin planted, cultivated and harvested and threshed the crop, and the scribes measured the grain in wooden tubs before it was emptied into the silos. Our bushel measure derives from this method. This meticulous method of recording was the basis of determining the quantity which each person in the whole nation would receive, the highest in the land receiving the most generous portion, the fellahin, as a matter of course, the least. Since everyone depended upon the Pharaoh for his sustenance, and because individual freedom really had no meaning, the chief concern of the Pharaoh was to control his administration, and this he did through an enormous bureaucracy. The regional administrators became too powerful, and in 1,860 B.C. Sesostris III (the Great) sacked them all and re-established complete personal control. His scribes then became the most powerful individuals in the land, next to the priesthood in fact, just in the same manner as are accountants today.

Those who produced the food received no honour, but a good harvest led to the public honouring of the chief scribe when he presented his accounts for the year. This contempt for the peasant, which has lasted these 4,000 years or more, has been the cause of a traditional indifference to the position of man in the biosphere, as well as to the function of the soil as part of the ecosphere. This indifference has resulted in the treatment of the soil as a raw product in a manufacturing process. Although such treatment proved the cause of the downfall of empires and civilisations in the past, there is little evidence that a change in outlook is taking place, even today. Pollution means, so far as propaganda is concerned, fumes and exhaust gases, smog, bottles and tin cans and other litter, but does not mean a diverted nutrient stream carrying poisons into the ecosystem, nor the exploitation of fields and animals by the use of chemicals and hormones.

Man's brief historical period, however, is marked by so many remarkable and laudable achievements, that his failure to appreciate the position of the soil as part of man's ecosphere might be forgiven, were it not for the associated denigration of the work of the peasant which sustains him. For example, it is recorded by Strabo, the Roman historian who travelled in Egypt in 25 B.C.

'The provinces of Old Egypt were divided into districts, these in turn into localities, and the smallest segments of these parts were the tillable fields. They needed to be marked out with great exactitude, for the Nile River removes and adds land every year, it constantly changes the ground, and also wipes out all signs that might serve to distinguish each man's property. Therefore, the Egyptians must repeat their measurements each year. The art of surveying is said to have developed out of this need, as arithmetic was developed by the Phoenicians to serve trade.'

He makes no mention of husbandry.

If we consider the ration of the Roman soldier which is in the record of the army of the great Scipio Africanus, we find that the corn ration (wheat) was 852 grams (approximately 30 oz); allowing for inedible portion, this would provide roughly 2,700 calories. The ration was doubled as a reward for heavy fighting. The troops made flat bread with coarse wheaten flour gristed in a portable mill, and they purchased when they could obtain them oil, onions, salt, garlic, radishes and wine. Every group of ten men carried on their transport mile one hand-mill and sufficient ration for 15 to 30 days, while each man carried approximately 8 lbs of grain, one pot and one drinking vessel. Meat was not part of the ration, and a small quantity only was consumed ritually on certain feast days.

The wheaten grain used was a hard variety containing probably between 14-16 per cent of protein. The food of the Roman peasant might have been varied by the occasional use of eggs, milk and cheese from time to time, but, unlike the wealthy classes whose luxurious banqueting has been the subject of report by historians and by contemporary writers, the fare of the ordinary Roman was of the simplest nature. Whole wheat bread and porridge, and olive oil were the main constituents.

The pattern of Roman agricultural history bears a significant resemblance to our present pattern of cereal food production and is worth relating briefly.

With the growth of the Roman military forces, and the consequent depletion of family labour, the small family farms were gradually bought by city magnates and worked as large estates by slave labour under the control of overseers. Thus it came about that the direct personal interest in the local problems of drainage, cultivation, rotation of crops, vagaries of the weather, etc. was lost. The production of grain fell off, and the land was given over in many instances to horticulture and viticulture. Cheap grain was imported from exploited colonies overseas, and doled out free to the dispossessed small farmers now crowding into Rome where they swelled the ranks of the unemployed. The wheat lands of North Africa were, in turn, converted into desert country in order to feed this vast population.

There is ample recorded evidence by Roman writers, to mention only Virgil, Horace, Columella, Pliny and Varro, that a high level of agricultural knowledge had previously existed, and that it was not being applied during the Imperial and the Principate periods. The result was erosion, the silting up of streams and drains, and the formation of swamps which later became malarial. Later attempts to colonise the conquered territories by soldier settlement were defeated by the same social forces. The tributary exactions of Rome laid on the Governors of the conquered regions descended as an oppressive burden of taxation on to the backs of the colonists, who, forced to exploit rather than apply the principle of crop rotation, exhausted the soil and finally abandoned their farms. In A.D. 60, Columella could write that 'the people of Latium would have died of starvation had it not been for imported corn.'

Considerable areas of the abandoned land of Latium and the Maremma ultimately became malarial swamps. Sardinia, Sicily, Spain and North Africa, once the granaries of a rapacious Rome, were finally exhausted. Hills were denuded of forest, and a mildly humid climate became that of an arid land. The bare hills and mountains of this classical region which the modern tourist observes, were made by man.

Sir William Ramsay who had made a detailed exploration of the region wrote the following in the *National Geographical Magazine* for 1922, as follows:

'[the Province of Asia] in Roman times was highly populated, and therefore highly cultivated . . . . It is difficult to give by statistics any conception of the great wealth and numerous population of Asia Minor in the Roman period. In the single province of 'Asia', to use the Roman name for the western part of the peninsula, which was the richest and most highly educated of the whole country, there were 230 cities which each struck its own special coinage, under its own name and its own magistrates; each proud of its individuality and character as a self-governing unit in the Great Empire.'

It is not only in Roman history that we find warning of the dangers facing us. Centuries before this the Greeks had also led the way to such soil destruction. Imagine you are listening to the words of Plato in 300 B.C.:

'There are mountains in Attica which can now keep nothing but bees, but which were clothed not very long ago, with fine trees producing timber suitable for roofing the largest buildings; and roofs hewn from this timber are still in existence. There were also many lofty trees, while the country produced boundless pastures for cattle. The annual supply of rainfall was not lost as it is at present, through being allowed to flow over the denuded surface into the sea, but was received by the country, in all its abundance, into her bosom, where she stored it in her impervious potter's earth, and so was able to discharge the drainage of the heights into the hollows in the form of springs and rivers with an abundant volume and a wide territorial distribution. The shrines that survive to the present day on the sites of extinct water supplies are evidence for the correctness of my present hypothesis.'

So pertinent are these comments in our present situation, that they could well have been delivered during the conference on water supplies at the Royal Society of Arts in 1971 (see page 35).

The U.S. Department of Agriculture, and many State Department experts, have recorded long-term detailed studies of the depletion of fertility and gross loss of the nation's soils, under the pressure of commercial wheat production. We have produced a voluminous and authoritative warning literature on this subject since 1926.

Australia has exported wheat to Britain for merely a century, and in

84

that short time has laid waste vast areas of once productive soil, only because financial rapacity took precedence over sound principles of husbandry.

What the Nile did for Egypt with its annual deposit of black silt, must be achieved in other lands by spreading plant and animal and human refuse or by crop rotation and mixed animal husbandry. This however is not so immediately lucrative as continuous monoculture, the final cost of which is passed on to posterity.

In the publication *Genetic Vulnerability of Major Crops,* issued by the U.S. National Research Council of the National Academy of Sciences 1972,it is reported that maize, which has become the greatest crop in the USA has already suffered in 1971 a 15 per cent overall destruction by fungus infestation (50 per cent destruction in Florida) owing to genetic vulnerability. By selective breeding to increase yield, protective genetic characters have been lost.

Maize achieved its greatest selective development at the hands of the Mayas in Central America over a period of some 300 years. Growing amongst these selected strains, however, was the wild Teosinte, from which it is believed that maize has been developed. The continued presence of Teosinte in Mexican maize fields is now credited with the supply of mixed genetic characters that have given the modern maize plant a renewal of valuable genetic qualities. Now, Teosinte is disappearing at an accelerating rate according to H.G. Wilkes.[5] Let us follow in another example the sort of activity that the 'forced draught' of economic exploitation of soils produces. To prevent cross-fertilisation – nature's method of ensuring survival – the tassles of the corn plant, which carry the fertilising pollen for the flowers that became ears of corn, used to be carefully pulled. This naturally called for intensive labour. When a Texas variety was found to be sterile, it became the desirable plant, because the labour of tassle pulling was dispensed with. By 1970, practically all corn crops in the USA were of the Texas variety. The potential for famine is ever present from fungus disease, the more so when we force yields at the expense of ecological balance.

In the USA over the period during which soil, agriculture and forestry experts have published their warnings, millions of small farmers have left the land for the cities. At the same time the great latifundias formed by merging the countless small-holdings, financed by insurance and conglomerate corporations and managed by agricultural 'experts' and economist accountants, are showing signs of collapse. Some indeed have already been liquidated.

In the *New York Times* of 1 June 1972, there was a report on the productivity of American agriculture. Referring to the displacement of 1 million people from the land to the cities, the report says:

85

'Today's urban crisis is a consequence of failure in rural America. The Land Grant Colleges cannot shoulder all the blame for that failure, but no single institution – private or public – has played a more crucial role. The Land Grant institutions' research has focused on projects that primarily aid agri-business, and the biggest producers such as the two-storey factory at Cornell that tests manufacturing methods for the processors, and elsewhere the development of big and costly planting and harvesting machinery.' The report refers to the Act of 1802 which established the Colleges for the 'education of children of farm and factory workers by endowment of Public Land', and the Amending Act of 1887 which further defined research basic to the problems of agriculture in its broadest aspects, and such 'investigations which have as their purpose, the development and improvement of rural home and rural life, and the maximum contribution by agriculture to the welfare of the consumer.' A semantic analysis of these words give ample scope for distortion of the original intention by an industrialised profit-oriented economy.

Continuing, the report states:
'That is where the Land Grant system has failed, it has abandoned its historic mission. Only 5 per cent of 6,000 man-years of annual research is people oriented.' Citing the annual Public Fund contribution of $750 billion to agricultural aims of the Colleges and experimental stations, the report states: 'The public has a right to expect that these intellectual and scientific researches be more than a subsidy for corporate agri-business.'

Projects primarily serving big producers include merchandising the harvest of twenty-five food crops from apples to tomatoes. Five separate colleges are investigating the harvesting of strawberries. Ohio State tested plastic-coated cartons for dairy products; Virginia Polytechnic factors affecting shelf life of sweet potato flakes; and Wisconsin a fast process to produce mozarella cheese 'mild, but satisfactory for normal uses'. 'Research of the absurd', to cite the report, included 'correct methods for squeezing a grapefruit, attempts to breed a seedless cucumber, and to cross cauliflower with broccoli', plus, believe it or not, 'a Cornell study on the cleaning of dogs' teeth, sponsored by Superior Pet Products; development and care of golf course grasses, and athletic field turfs, and the heat retaining properties of artificial turf.'

'These "researches",' the report said, 'are playing around with games while rural America falls apart.'

The report states that such few researches that have been made into problems of rural life are 'aimless, repetitions of analyses of rural conditions that tend to irrelevant studies of characteristics'. The University of Tennessee study, 'to determine the relationship of education to migration' and a Missouri study 'the typologies of poverty among rural people' are examples of this.

The implication for the rural poor, continues the report, are 'If they stay in rural America, a rural sociologist will come around every now and then to poke at them with surgery.'

The report entitled 'Hard Tomatoes, Hard Times', is the result of six months study by twelve investigators financed by the Field Foundation, and sponsored by the Centre for Community Change. It will be the basis of a law suit planned by the Agri-business Accountability Project against public and educational officials involved, as well as of a Senate Committee Hearing.

By strange coincidence, the *New York Times* of May 31, carried a headline banner on the Woman's Page: 'What's Gone Wrong with the Tomato?' Quoted at the head of a half-page spread are these words from the First Deputy Commissioner, New York City Department of Consumer Affairs: 'Tomatoes used to spurt driblets of red liquid, now you have to cut them with a saw, and then they just sort of sag quietly.' In the body of the article is the reported explanation from Dr Stewart Dallyn, Professor of Vegetable Crops, at Cornell University's Long Island Vegetable Research Station:

'In order for tomatoes to be picked by a machine, it was necessary to develop varieties resistant to rough handling, that are much firmer, and in the eyes of many people who like to think of tomatoes as large, juicy and relatively soft textured, not so good. The machines just can't pick this kind. Tomatoes are handled as hardware.'

Neither the farmer with direct interest in the quality of his product as a foodstuff, nor the consumer who is interested in food savour, has any place in agri-business.

Prof. Dallyn represents a whole generation of agricultural scientists with this outlook, not only in the USA but everywhere in Western civilisation, and they are advising the underdeveloped countries how to undermine both their societies and their nutritional health.

'Too many potatoes sold to the consumer are scabby, cracked, damaged, misshapen, green, difficult to prepare, of poor quality, tasteless or simply inedible' runs a report of the Consumers' Committee for Great Britain, presented to Mr Prior, Minister of Agriculture, in June 1972. This confirms a public statement made by the Manager of Sainsbury's Stores, that 33 per cent of potatoes received by his firm have to be rejected for poor quality. This is another example of the nutritional price paid (a hidden cost) for economic agri-business.

How can quality be maintained when the natural cycle of soil fertility is ignored. In a cycle of good husbandry, it has long been appreciated that leguminous crops restore fertility to the soil, a fact we seem to have forgotten. The Roman poets record this fact, but the knowledge of why this is so was not revealed until the close of the nineteenth century. Hellriegel and Willfarth then discovered that these plants live in symbiotic relationship with soil bacteria which are capable of 'fixing' atmospheric nitrogen in the nodules which they produced on the roots of leguminous plants. This was a memorable discovery which would have had a revolutionary impact on agriculture, had it not been for the burgeoning science of chemistry, which, more in tune with the materialistic philosophy of contemporary science, diverted attention to the use of soluble nitrate as a fertiliser.

REFERENCES

1. Braidwood, R., *Man and the Ecosphere,* Freeman, 1971
2. Mangelsdorf, P.C., McNeish, R.S., and Willey, G., *Handbook of Mid-American Indians,* vol.1, University of Texas Press, 1964
3. Byers, D.S. (ed.), *Pre-History of Techuacan Valley,* University of Texas Press, 1968
4. Jacob, H.E., *6,000 Years of Bread,* Doubleday Doran, 1945
5. Wilkes, H.G., *Science,* 22 September 1972

10. REPRODUCTIVE MAN

'In ancient times people were few and wealthy and without strife. People at present think that five sons are not too many, and each son has five sons also, and before the death of the grandfather there are already twenty-five descendants. Therefore people are more and wealth is less, they work hard and receive little. The life of a nation depends upon people having enough food, not upon the number of people.'

Han Fei-Tzu, Chou dynasty, *c.* 500 B.C.

'The strongest witness is the vast population of the earth to which we are a burden, and she scarcely can care for our needs: as our demands grow greater, our complaints against Nature's inadequacy are heard by all. The scourges of pestilence, famine, wars, and earthquakes have come to be regarded as a blessing to overcrowded nations, since they serve to prune away the luxuriant growth of the human race.'

Tertullian: *De Anima* (concerning the soul), *c.* 160-230 A.D.

Already in 1930, Raymond Pearl had drawn attention to the fact that there was statistical evidence that human populations, like those of the lemmings, voles and elephants, tend to be self-regulating in size. At that date there was ample support for the conclusion that populations of small creatures like the fruit fly, amoebae and so on, were in fact self-regulating, but in the case of man, there were conflicting influences that had to be identified and their effects isolated. Pearl[1] and his colleagues had done this. Excluding such influences as migration, food supply, economic conditions, social forces, etc., there remained birth-rate and death-rate, natality and mortality. Pearl emphasised the importance of expressing these as a ratio, rather than in crude figures. This ratio he termed the Vital Index, i.e. $\dfrac{\text{births} \times 100}{\text{deaths}}$.

When this ratio was applied to the available statistics for births and deaths in England and Wales from 1838-1920, it emerges that although the general birth-rate per ten thousand for the period fell from 310 to 255, with a peak around 250 in 1875, the Vital Index rose steadily. This is best seen when expressed as a graph taken from Pearl's paper.

When Pearl and others had been making their investigations, the

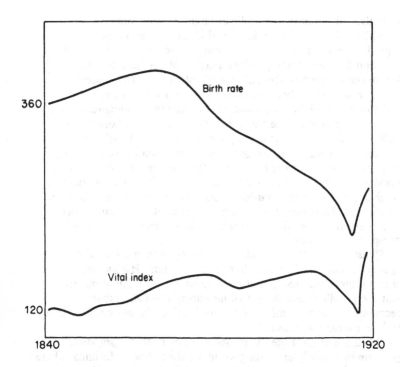

Fig 12. *Trend of vital index and crude death rate England and Wales 1838-1926. (Redrawn from Pearl, R.,* Human Biology and Racial Welfare, *Lewis, London 1930.)*

falling birth-rate was an occasion for prophets of doom to deplore the position, but already two babies were being born for every death, compared with 1·4 at the beginning of 1839. Numerically, therefore, and apart from all other biological trends, the survival rate was constantly rising and over this long period there operated a quite striking self-regulation of the population.

Pearl also cited the same figures for France, from 1901-1925, and was able to demonstrate the same phenomenon, even after including the steep fall of the Vital Index for the war years 1914-18. The post-war increase, with quite astonishing rapidity, restored the even course of the Vital Index.

It had already been noted in the early nineteenth century that populations of organisms grew slowly at first, then accelerated in multiplication, and finally established a slow rate of increase. Verhulst,[2] a Belgian mathematician, was able to show that all such growth rates followed a logistic or sigmoid curve. Pearl and his co-workers, unaware of the existence of this work, rediscovered this

91

formula, and found that it applied to human populations.

Whilst it is reassuring to discover that self-regulation applies to our reproductive and survival rates, nothing is revealed as to the social situation that may develop before a degree of equilibrium is attained! Furthermore, the full effect of controls of endemic and epidemic disease is only recently becoming evident on a world scale, and the point of self-regulation may well be advanced to 'standing-room only'.

In a series of extensive experiments on a variety of Norway rat, Calhoun[3] discovered that the population seemed to be self-limiting, although there was no shortage of food. These animals were housed in an arena with complex approaches to feed and nesting boxes, which provided observational evidence of behaviour. There is a commentary on this work by Garrett Hardin, perhaps the most perceptive biologist of our time. He considers that Calhoun's rats suffered from 'information overload' as population increased within a circumscribed and complex environment.

Whilst the results of animal studies are open to question when applied without qualification to human situations, Hardin maintains that it is more than likely that restrictions in the supply of material and energy will be less likely to limit human population than this recondite problem of 'information overload'. Or, as one observer terms it, 'the ignorance explosion'.

One can best illustrate the complex nature of the information problem in a rapidly expanding world, by the following formula, where the symbol n = the number of elements of information involved:

$$1 + 2 + 3 \ldots (n - 1) + n = \frac{n(n-1)}{2}$$

Simply expressed, communication between two individuals involves only one relationship. Between 3 individuals, 3 relationships, with 4 the relationship becomes 6 (not 4) and with 5, there are 10, and so on. When the number becomes very large, the relationship becomes roughly proportional to the square of n, n^2. Thus, the attempt of an individual in a rapidly expanding world, to know the same proportion of what was happening in a simpler static world, such as that of around 1900, leads to 'information overload', with all its psychological consequences.

Recent published work of Krebs and associates on population studies of periodic rapid breeders such as the lemmings at Bear Lake, Canada, and the California vole, have led to the conclusion that there are definitely other factors besides predators or food limitation that operate to check certain rapidly reproducing animal populations.

Rangers in the Kenya National Park have recently reported this phenomenon with the African elephant. Countless animals, birds and

92

even insects, make use of restrictive mating rituals or patterns, that have a limiting effect on their numbers and a selective effect upon breeding. The Australian aboriginal, a Palaeolithic man, similarly utilises a tribal totem pattern of mating, which ensures the same result in a hostile environment.

But where do we stand in relation to this vexed question of over-population? Let us look at the views recently expressed by the Chairman of the Engineering Department of Carleton University, Ottawa, before the New York Academy of Science, on 23 February 1972. His paper is entitled 'The Ignorance Explosion'. Professor Lukasciewicz begins his discourse with a brief résumé of the facts which led him to make the study, namely over-population, depletion of natural resources, and of course pollution. The control of these three phenomena alone demands action at every level of social organisation from the local, national to international. Lukasciewicz however perceived that population problems are not entirely problems of matter and energy supply, they become, particularly in a period of rapid expansion, problems of information transfer, which is a product of an interlacing network of relationships between the elements of a highly industrialised system.

Human intelligence would appear to be definitely limited, although there are obvious difficulties in measuring its capacity. We can best express this concept by examining Man's evolution. It would be fair to assume that human intelligence developed in relation to the need for learning from experience and for making limited forecasts. The hominid that developed into man over a period of from 3-5 million years was faced with problems of survival of a unique kind. He was neither particularly powerful, armed with fangs or claws, nor was he fleet of foot, although he evolved in a savannah type of environment. He seems to have developed the use of weapons and group co-operation, and to have relied on memory for forecasting his strategy.

The time period necessary for this development is counted in millions of years. Civilised man is only some 10,000 years old, and scientifically technological man barely 150 years old! It is therefore not unreasonable to assume that evolutionary development of intelligence is inadequate to deal with the rapidly accelerating man-made dynamic change in our present Western civilisation. We have to make use of the same intelligence with which we have managed to deal with agricultural, pastoral and handicraft problems and their associated commerce for centuries past. It might be added as a footnote that man's lack of physical equipment and corresponding vulnerability formed the basis for his reproductive habits, in order to ensure the survival of the race.

An observation made by Sir William Hamilton in the first half of the nineteenth century first drew attention to the possible limits of immediate memory, and therefore of intelligence. He demonstrated that it was difficult to scan, in one operation, more than six marbles thrown upon the floor. Although this is a perceptual rather than a mental test it can be converted into the latter as Joseph Jacobs did in 1877, by using digits instead of objects. He found that the maximum number of digits that a normal man could repeat was seven or eight. The well-known Binet Test of intelligence, is based upon this observation.

Carrying this type of investigation further, more recently, Norbert Wiener (the father of cybernetics) and Claude Shannon (the psychologist) developed a mathematical theory of communication. This provides a precise measure of information carried when the digits of Jacob's Test, and their substitution by letters, or by syllables, or words, are used. Manifestly the use of seven or eight memorised items of this sort may each carry much condensed information. This is the added range given to early hominid intelligence by the invention of speech, and finally, of the written word.

Table 1: Span of Immediate Memory

Binary (1 bit)	Decimal (3·3 bits)	Alphabetic (4·7 bits)	Syllabic (10 bits)
110100	4972	XIR	for, line
0100110	86515	AYCZ	nice, it act
10010011	021942	EDLYG	time, who, to air
101100010	3776380	QIPEVT	by, west, cent, of, law

This table, copied from Miller demonstrates the fact that immediate memory depends more upon the number of items to be memorised than upon the information carried by each item. Binary digits carry one 'bit' of information. A good immediate memory can recall the order to nine binary digits, or seven decimal digits, six letters or five words.

The table, shows at a glance the basis for coding by symbols rich in information, and, at the same time, the limited capacity of human intelligence to make use of the coding through immediate memory. Whilst this is but one aspect of intellectual limitation, it shows the limitation to man's ability efficiently to codify information, i.e. to perceive 'laws governing complex phenomena', to recognise and to formulate complex variables in the form of neat packages of information, suffers under precisely the same mental disabilities.

A further and severe limit to intelligence is that imposed by the physiology of the nervous input mechanism itself. Depending on the type of stimulus to the input system, vision, hearing, etc., it seems that approximately seven different pieces of information among the mass of stimuli from the environment can be identified and transmitted. As before, this quantity, carried by the nerve channel,can be expanded by effective codifying, but the limits are still physiologically fixed.

The Ignorance Explosion, therefore, is the Information Explosion seen from the limited capacity of human intelligence. Two major factors are involved, the rapid increase in quantity and complexity of the man-made industrial environment, including numbers of people, their feeding, housing, transport, education, medical aid, etc., and the present realisation that the ecosphere with its feed-back networks is even more complex. Lukasciewicz,as an engineer, selects only one basic aspect of this highly complex matrix for close analysis. He concludes that because science since the eighteenth century has been the basis of technology and modern industry, a quantitative study of the relevant aspects of science may give us some measure, however indirect, of the mounting complexity of the modern industrial environment.

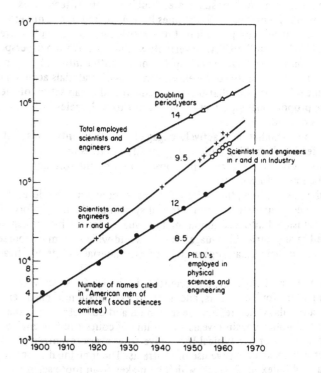

Fig 13. *The growth of the scientific population in the United States*

To this end, he examines growth, specialisation, obsolescence, immediacy, and complexity as those aspects of organised science which, in his view, demonstrate increasing human incapacity to 'grasp' the available scientific information, let alone cope with a science based social environment.

For example: slums are associated with poverty, therefore slums are a cause of poverty, therefore spend billions of dollars on slum clearance. After this has been done it is found that that condition called poverty still persists, and a re-examination of the problem becomes belatedly necessary, the more clearly to define the meaning of 'poverty'. Lewis,[6] who chose to live for some time in the slums himself, has recently described a 'culture of poverty'. Underdeveloped countries are poor because they have no investment capital; they have no capital because they are poor; therefore supply aid in the form of capital. They become poorer.

The Royal Society of London published in March 1664 the first scientific journal, and since 1760 the number of scientific journals has been increasing at a constant rate, doubling every fifteen years. Several minor reports of similar studies have appeared in recent years in Europe, but this compilation of Lukasciewicz is more complete even if it deals only with the USA. Nevertheless, and again from our perspective viewpoint, already at the end of the nineteenth century, Helmholtz could write, 'I have noticed the enormous mass of materials accumulated by Science. It is obvious that the arrangement and organisation of them must be proportionally perfect, if we are not to be hopelessly lost in the mass of erudition.'

Everyone who has been actively engaged in both scientific research and professional teaching during the past fifty years is only too painfully aware of the force of that observation by the foremost scientific mind of his century.

At the present time, the United Nations is sponsoring the development of a computer storage and retrieval system in which all information will be translated into a common 'metalanguage', from which it can be retrieved in any current language! Such a world-wide system of course, involves an initial human organisation of the material and its codification.

The number of engineers and scientists in the USA also shows a doubling every fourteen years, and a recent examination of engineering school curricula, which reflect the dynamics and obsolescence in that field of technology, again reveals a doubling of courses in five engineering departments of five typical U.S. universities every seventeen years.

Scientists make extensive use of abstracts. The individual scientist keeps a card index of abstracts which he makes from those scientific papers which, during his reading of current literature, impress him as being of value to his work. Obviously this is restricted to his limited field of study. Should he wish to scan a larger field, he reverses the procedure, and refers to abstract journals, or indexes, first, and then seeks out the original papers.

As the number of published researches multiplies, so the abstracting journals multiply also, and, by 1963 according to Lukasciewicz, they had reached the staggering figure of 1,855, doubling every fifteen years. These are U.S. figures but it is reasonable to assume a parallel European rate of growth.

The Physico-chemical Tables by Landolt Bornstein appeared first in 1870. Von Helmholtz expressed his concern in the last decade of the nineteenth century when there were only ten abstracting publications in existence.

The close approximation of the growth rate of scientific publications and of the number of scientists seems to confirm that there is a biological limit to intelligence. If the number of scientists increased relatively to the increase of population one might fairly assume an increase in intelligence. Furthermore, it seems to be the case that the growth of specialisation follows the same trend, that is if the degree of specialisation can be expressed as the ratio

$$\frac{\text{number of scientific journals or total quantity of information}}{\text{quantity per scientist}}$$

since it doubles every fifteen years. In the field of medicine, it is only too evident that specialisation has proceeded to such a degree that few medical graduates deal with the patient as a human being.

We are dealing with complexity of information, not quantity of information, when we discuss specialisation. As shown mathematically at the beginning of this chapter, the increase in complexity takes place at a greater rate than the growth of information. Applying that formula, as the quantity of information rises from 1 to 32 in 5 doubling periods, complexity increases to 5 billion.

It must not be forgotten that scientific knowledge is not the only field of complexity. Our formula can be applied to the complexity of our modern industrial societies with industrial production, distribution, communication, agencies and institutions of government, trade unions, fuel and power, water and sewerage. Add the complex interaction between these components with those of the ecosphere and one begins to have an idea of how terrifying the situation is.

But our engineer contributor has not yet finished with us. He introduces two other sources of difficulty, the immediacy of information and its obsolescence. Obsolescence is the obverse of immediacy, and the term is better applied to technology and engineering, where above-mentioned studies of curricula show the increasing obsolescence of knowledge from the time of a student's graduation.

Everyone knows the quip about the specialist being a person who knows more and more about less and less, but not everyone has had his attention directed to the degree of total unspecialised 'grasp' that could be possible for a superintellect. Hermann von Helmholtz during his lifetime, 1821-1892, thoroughly encompassed the fields of physiology, pathology, anatomy, physics, optics, acoustics, thermo-dynamics, electro-dynamics, and medicine. No modern Helmholtz could possibly manage such a conspectus.

I am indebted to the New York Academy of Science and to Professor Lukasciewicz for permission to make use of his material, and in particular for his diagrammatic illustration of the degree of 'grasp' relative to the total volume of information available. We are all aware of the recourse made by politicians to committees of experts. The trouble is that the experts, or specialists, while they are eminently capable of dealing with their specialised problems, lack the overall 'grasp' or comprehension that is essential when dealing with problems of environment or of human society. Here we are face to face with the practical outcome of the ignorance explosion.

As we have seen, the growth both in volume and complexity of information, has become extremely rapid, and a concomitant of this is its immediacy. This mass of information which is increasing at accelerating rate demands a correspondingly increasing fraction of the time available for even the best intellects to assimilate. And when I write the word 'best' I realise just how much the term 'best' and the term 'assimilate' actually mean. Consider now the diagram.

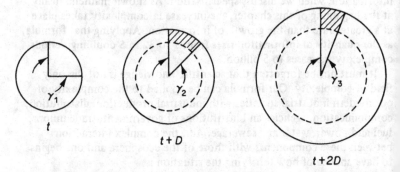

Fig 14. *Graphic representation of the 'ignorance explosion'. The area of each circle represents the total information available at time intervals equal to the doubling period.*

98

Suppose the areas of the three circles represents the total amount of information available at three different periods of time separated by two intervals of time, during each of which the total amount of information has doubled. Obviously the area of the second circle will be twice that of the first, and the area of the third 4 times that of the 1st circle. Mathematically expressed these times are represented by t, $t + d$, $t + d$, where d means double.

The segments of the circle cut out by the two radii represent the intellectual capacity of Man, and since this is limited, the areas of these segments remains constant, but the angle between the radii gets smaller. Let these angles be called 1, 2, 3, and let us use these angles as a measure of the degree of 'grasp'. The reciprocals of these values, i.e. $\frac{1}{1}$ $\frac{1}{2}$ $\frac{1}{3}$ are measures of the degree of specialisation.

The circles represented by the broken lines mark out a ring the area of which represents the increase of information added during the doubling periods. The shaded sections of these rings represents the new information added within a given speciality, that has in fact displaced obsolete information. If the angles 1, 2 and 3 are compared, it will at once be evident that the degree of 'grasp' has diminished rapidly.

Quite clearly these considerations apply not only to verifiable physical data, but also to those of an unpredictable non-verifiable human situation. The calculations of opposing general staffs in time of war are based on relatively better verifiable facts, and the catastrophic results are there for all to see, even if they never profit therefrom. Panels of leading economists make predictions of the same order of accuracy. No—man's environmental situation is verifiable after the event, and has limited, if any, value for prediction.

Could it be that the failure of the application of modern, highly sophisticated, mathematical techniques for handling environmental problems is due to the limitations of the intelligence that uses them? A good example is that of Systems Theory, which originally was an abstract field of mathematical study.

Some very outspoken criticism of systems method has been made. Two of these are quoted by Professor Lukasciewicz. The U.S. Assistant Secretary for Transportation in 1968 told a research forum that,

'if systems analysis cannot provide some immediate inputs to the decisions and plans which will be made over the next 2-3 years, starting as of yesterday, it will miss out on the most important single set of transportation decisions that will ever have been made in the United States. .... The time is now, and models completed and perfected in 1972 will have missed the bus.'

Any system of information treatment is only as effective as the intellectual capacity of those who apply it. Our lack of comprehension of the nature of the factors involved, and of their interaction, is the source of our failure efficiently to apply highly sophisticated mathematical techniques.

Dr Moynihan, while head of the Council of Urban Affairs, emphasised that it was first essential to discover precisely what the urban crisis was all about. 'We have difficulties we don't understand. . . . It is simply not enough to want to do good. We've outgrown our ability to deliver on our promises.'

Perhaps, just as population seeems to be self-limiting, but not before grave social disturbance is manifest, so science may be self-limiting as Lukasciewicz seems to demonstrate from his selected data. The rate of intensity of scientific research certainly appears to be diminishing.

I would like at this point to state my own opinion of the cause of this 'ignorance explosion'. It seems to me that all these trends are due to the fact that our economic dogma is at the root of the technological misuse of science, man and his environment. Instead of speculating as to how, biologically, to improve Man's intelligence, or how, technolo-gically, to devise a super-intelligence machine, we should perhaps enquire into the causes of dynamic change in the human environment. Daily our ears and eyes are presented with terms such as 'standard of living', 'expanding economy', 'economic growth-rate', and the 'GNP'. These articles of belief of the economist's approach to human affairs have become the directing influence of our industrial civilisation. What is more, the same economic system that stokes the fires of 'growth' has, until yesterday, boasted a spurious advance of prosperity by ignoring the social costs and the costs of depletion of resources as well as environmental destruction.

An ecosystem, as we have seen, is one in which energy and 'order' introduced from solar radiation are cycled so that the most efficient use is made of the input. The final degradation products are recycled throughout the system. The closer one examines such ecosystems, the more obvious it becomes that the biomass (the living component) which functions in such systems, is so integrated by feed-back responses as to extract every last available quantum of energy and of molecular order. I am convinced that civilised man is today in a position to profit from biological knowledge to much greater advantage than he gained from the application of physical science to technology. Briefly expressed, he is being made aware of the road to survival. In this connection it is interesting to recall that from 1929 into the 'fifties, the distinguished physicist J.D. Bernal was writing books concerned with the social implication of physical science, and that during this period another scientist, Lancelot Hogben, became a figure of world stature with the

100

publication of *Mathematics for the Millions*. This was followed by *Science for the Citizen*, and the American publisher Alfred Knopf, with post-Colombian optimism, printed on the title page 'The first and second primers for the age of plenty.' Hogben also was deeply concerned with the social implications of science, and these two books are masterpieces of exposition intended for Mr Everyman.

In his first book, *The World, the Flesh and the Devil*, Bernal wrote 'Normal man is an evolutionary dead-end; mechanical man, apparently a break in inorganic evolution, is actually more in the tradition of a further evolution.'

Bernal, the physicist and Hogben the biologist were both writing at the period during which it was obvious to any thinking person that the fabric of industrial civilisation was threatened with disaster. Both of them held to the faith in scientific knowledge as the saviour of mankind. In actual fact, the real driving force is not science, but economics, and economics involves us all personally.

Van Rensselaer Potter,[6] with commendable optimism, sees a way out of this impasse by the application of what he terms 'biocybernetics' as a link between economics and ecology.

Potter, who is assistant director of a cancer research institute, became increasingly impressed with the state of cellular disorder which is known as cancer, and the analogous phenomena of disorder in social life. This 'subconscious drive' as he calls it, led him to put a number of disparate thoughts together under the title of 'Bio-ethics'. His conclusion appears to be that cybernetics, which is the mathematical formulation of rules governing feed-back phenomena, and which is the basis of computer science, could be used to bring about co-operation between the ecologist and the economist.

He frankly states that such a bio-cybernetic approach must be survival-orientated, not profit-orientated. Potter may well have foreshadowed the application of such a synthetic approach, for as stated above eco-systems are the most efficient converters of matter and energy, and the economist is, apart from his preoccupation with profit, by definition concerned with the same efficient use of matter and energy.[7]

But even at this stage of the application of cybernetics via computers to industrial production, we are witnessing some appalling end results. Hundreds of thousands of motor vehicles are being recalled to have mechanical or material faults rectified. In June 1972, 84,000 new models were recalled in the United States by one of the major manufacturers. The fenders collapsed when a lifting jack was applied. This apparently trivial fault reveals a much more fundamental weakness. The highly computerised control both of the production line and of the design and specification of materials used in construction, seems to show that Lukasciewicz's pessimism is well founded.

Notwithstanding this sort of error, which may in fact be only another result of the 'forced draught' due to the profit motive in economic calculations in the accounts branch of industry, the principle of cybernetics is the only one available to us in complex ecological systems. It will be useful to examine for a moment the origins of Potter's ideas as he carried out his laborious and meticulous physiological investigations of cancer research.

Cells, the ultimate living units that together form an organ of the body, can be cultivated artificially in appropriate nutrient fluid, the composition and physical conditions of which are kept under rigid control. But they are what Potter calls 'idio cells', that is they are alive, but their activity is without constructive 'purpose'. The same cells living as part of an organism do not simply multiply indefinitely, they come under 'restraints' imposed by the structures of which they form a part. These restraints in large part derive from their interaction with each other, as well as with cells of other organs.

More recently, in his characteristic style, Szent Györgyi, Nobel Laureate in biochemistry, had this to say about the physiology of the muscle cell.

'The more we know about muscle, the less we understand it, and it looks as though we would soon know everything, and would understand nothing. The situation is the same in most other biological processes, and pathological conditions such as the degenerative diseases. This suggests that some very basic information is missing.'

The striking thing about cancer cells, which are cells of the organ that are growing without restraint, demanding increasing blood supply (food) and invading other tissues of the body, is that they too are idiot cells. They no longer form part of a system with negative, i.e. restraining, feed-back. Their disorder, by comparison with the order of normal tissue cells, was, for Potter, the stimulus to his thought about bio-cybernetics. He was well aware that others had been struck by the same thought, and had looked upon man's activities as disordered, with respect to the natural environment.

Berrill, a noted Canadian biologist, and an authority on organismal growth and development, as long ago as 1955 likened man to a cancer cell,[8] whose overgrowth and greedy unthinking demands would ultimately destroy himself and his environment. It is 150 years since William Cobbett, enraged at the depopulation of rural England by industrial urbanisation, stigmatised London as 'the Great Wen', a wen being a tumour growth. The thought is not new, even if the scientific basis for it is today more sophisticated. I have no doubt that outlying citizens of the Roman Empire thought the same about Rome. They certainly had good reason to do so.

There is indeed a discomforting aspect of this analogy between urbanised industrial man and a tumour cell. It is this. All other living creatures have their predators which check propagation of the unfit (those too slow, too weak, or too old to escape); excepting the pathogenic micro-organisms and viruses, man has no predator except perhaps himself, and his preoccupation with the development of ever more potent weapons of destruction could be seen by some as an aspect of the same phenomenon.

Nobel Laureate physicist, Hannes Alfven, and his wife have dealt with the population explosion and the Expectation Explosion,[9] but although their essay reveals their full appreciation of the ignorance explosion, they do not specifically categorise it. On the other hand, their summary of the expectation explosion reveals the contradictions inherent in the present human situation. They point to the facts of vastly increased production of consumer goods and of foodstuffs, greater freedom of speech and liberty of action, and ever-increasing expectation of more of these to come, and yet, contemporaneously even greater limitation of freedom and greater extent of poverty, and even semi-starvation than ever before.

The Alfvens clearly discern the dehumanisation of society arising from its industrial complexity, which is a function of increasing numbers and mounting problems of industrial origin. This kind of society they term 'cybernetic' and whilst they obviously accept the idea of progress, they deplore the incapacity of men in positions of power to cope with such social disasters as are continually reported in the daily press. As one reads this fascinatingly brilliant survey of *Living on the Third Planet*, one is impressed by the humanity of the authors, and by the feeling of despair that they disclose in their analysis. Whilst the Alfvens deplore the ignorance of power groups of individuals in an industrial society, Lukasciewicz offers no escape from the ignorance explosion either, as he considers it inherent in the industrial society.

He provides us with tangible evidence of trends which could be halted if not reversed, and, I am sufficiently sanguine to consider that basic actions might be taken, perhaps belatedly, but nevertheless in part effectively.

As the Alfvens demonstrate, action on a global scale could stop the population increase within two years. This, however, is wishful thinking. Of course such global action will not, and could not be organised. On the other hand, the alleged necessity for 'economic growth' could be erased by Western civilisations acting in concert. So also could their population growth be controlled by them at the same time.

Returning to Raymond Pearl's important contributions of almost fifty years ago, we are able to review this work in the light of what has happened since. The underdeveloped countries, or the countries not yet fully exploited in the name of economic progress, have demonstrated an upsurge of population that is the real basis for the term 'explosion'. According to United Nations statistics, these countries hold 69 per cent of the adult population of the world, and 80 per cent of its children and adolescents. This, as Dr Seitz pointed out is perhaps the most important factor causing increasing impoverishment and retarding rational development of those countries. He and others, contend that this is because the medical and hygienic revolution preceded the attempts to improve the economies by aid from industrial countries.

There is an opposite opinion which places the responsibility for increased population on economic progress, pointing to the fact that the Scandinavian countries in the nineteenth century showed the same excessive upsurge in population before medical science had started to exert any influence. As indicated at the beginning of this section, since Pearl and his associates could come to a firm conclusion only after all the various conflicting influences had been given careful, statistical assessment more careful work is needed to decide where the responsibility lies. Kingsley Davis, a modern demographer, is one of those who places the responsibility on medical science, and provides ample basis for his conclusion.

Whatever the reasons, what we are witnessing is an overgrowth of population in circumstances where one would suppose natural restraints would operate, such as in the impoverished farming regions of Latin America where people are compelled to migrate to already overcrowded cities in hope of finding some means of subsistence.

As Pearl demonstrated, the decreasing death-rate, unless followed by a similar trend in birth-rate, leads to sharp increase in population. What makes the situation so grave is that in so many countries simultaneously such trends have reached a point where any extensive disruption of food supply by drought, pandemic of fungous disease of grain crops, or some natural disaster on a large scale, could upset an already unstable balance between life and death.

Whilst it may be true that population is self-regulating what will happen in the meantime before this principle asserts itself?

Elsewhere I have mentioned the application of 'systems mathematics' on solutions of such complex and variable orders as an ecosystem. There are leading biologists such as Bertalanffy and Weiss who argue strongly that this is at least a hopeful approach to the biology of cellular organisation in living things. Accepting the caution that mathematics is a tool for dealing with facts, and that it is the ability adequately to use the tool that sets its limits, we should consider, if only briefly, the recent report of the Club of Rome. Controversy concerning the results notwithstanding, the question is, not the

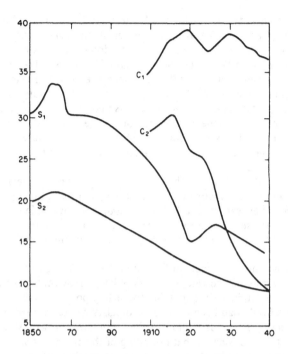

Fig 15. *A comparison of birth and death rate trends in Scandinavia, S1 and S2, and Ceylon C1 and C2 respectively. It is evident that in the former country, prior to industrial development the birth-rate was already falling faster than the death-rate. In Ceylon, on the contrary, the birth-rate has continued at a high level, and the death-rate, owing to the application of scientific medical principles has fallen precipitously.*

correctness of the projection of the date of Doomsday, but rather the nature of the facts examined and the trends revealed.

In 1968 Aurelio Pecci, the one-time chief of the Olivetti calculating and typewriting machine company, and now head of a management consultant firm, Italconsult, founded the Club, together with Kogaro Uemura, President of the Economic Federation of Japan, and Alexander King, Director-General of the British Office of Economic Co-operation. One would suppose that such a powerfully representative group of economists would at least be biased in favour of an optimistic assessment of the world economic situation. We should bear in mind Professor Lukasciewicz's definition of 'grasp' when reading that Pecci is reported as saying by way of explanation of this research project that 'We needed something to make mankind's predicament more easy to grasp'. Supported by a substantial grant of $250,000 from the Volkswagen Foundation in 1970, Dr Pecci's group elicited the aid of the top-level

105

computer experts at the Massachusetts Institute of Technology, the birthplace of cybernetics and of the computer. At MIT under the direction of Professor J. Forrester, Dennis Meadows, a computer expert, set to work on Pecci's problem – that of human survival. The selection of MIT was almost predetermined because Prof. Forrester had been engaged on the development of a species of giant computer that could simulate all the major ecological factors operating in the human ecosphere. Remembering the cautionary note above, and bearing in mind the fact that this investigation was conducted by computer experts in the home of cybernetics, a balanced approval of the conclusions is warranted.

The kind of data with which these 'systems' experts had to deal included the interacting factors of population, food production, arable land areas with their varying productivities, sources of available energy and material, fertilisers, chemical weedicides, pesticides, tractors, transport, pollution, etc., and industrial production of these latter items.

There was an enormous mass of factual material relating to the sources of materials and power, rates of population growth, types and degrees of pollution, including that due to nuclear power. Hitherto, inspired guesses only had been made by ecologists. Some considered that the 'Spaceship Earth' as Boulding called it, would end with standing room only. Others considered that poisoning of the ecosphere would spell Doomsday. Meadows and his collaborators, working with Forrester's computer, came up with a different answer. Depletion of non-renewable resources would, in all probability, bring to an end the consumer civilisation so wantonly enjoyed at present by the affluent societies in particular. It should be remarked that these results are published in a report entitled *The Limits to Growth*.

Whether the crisis point will be reached by the year 2020, as the results of the exercise appear to predict, or, 2070, or 3000, the trend of the correlated data remains the same. Resources will become ever scarcer as industrialisation grows, and growth of industrialisation is central to our present mode of economic thinking. With growing scarcity of resources, capital will tend to be expended in increasing quantities on materials, and in diminishing amount upon plant and development. That ever-present spectre, population overgrowth, will finally confirm the prognostication of Malthus, and almost coterminously, industry and food production will fail to keep the artificial balancing act in being.

The MIT team, like wrestlers trying to escape from Half-Nelson grips, fed other possible escape systems into their computer. Even at present undiscovered but estimated data on resources were fed into it, with the result that overwhelming pollution then ruined the biosphere, i.e. the living part of the ecosphere. New methods of preventing this destruction of the biosphere were proposed, but the cybernetic response was 'overpopulation and starvation'. There were, moreover, grave social consequences of improving technology, such as unemployment of unmanageable proportions.

Countless 'scenarios' as runs the jargon of cybernetic analysis, were fed into the computer, with only one result — 'all growth projections end in collapse'.

The MIT team does however come up with constructive solutions to the problem of the fate of industrial man. The first has, of course, been long since advocated, and recently again by the Alfvens, namely global concerted effort to control birth-rate with the object of obtaining equal rates of births and deaths. In a corresponding manner they recommend that industrial plant should only replace existing plant, and not extend it.

The MIT programme also calls for a 'change in behaviour patterns'. I prefer the advocacy of a fundamental change in moral outlook; but whichever term you prefer, the object is to stop the pursuit of production *per se*, and to replace inbuilt obsolescence with durability and simplicity of repair. The idea of industrial 'stagnation', is anathema to many people. Yet the present course will lead into the morass of ultimate stagnation, where we will sink in any case.

A Utopian idea? No doubt, if only because of the appalling difficulties facing any attempt to control population. Consider only the political fear hidden in the minds of those in power at such a course.

However, as Yoicha Kaya, a systems analyst in Geneva at the Batelle Institute and a member of the Club of Rome, expressed it to a *Time Magazine* reporter, 'The report makes one thing abundantly clear: there is a limit to everything. There is no use wringing hands. We can, and we must try to do what is humanly possible, and we must act soon.'

The MIT group does put forward constructive proposals as well as a vigorous attack on the population problem. Anyone who has given time to the study of the population question must come to the conclusion that it is the crux of the matter. Unhappily there are prominent confusing voices which overlook the main issue. Whether there is a population crisis *now*, or whether it will come later begs the question. Continued growth of population will eventually defeat all other efforts to feed, clothe, house and service the mass of people.

The MIT group proceeds to recommend recycling of all waste materials, and the composting of all garbage. It advocates complete reversal of industrial practice where built-in obsolescence must be replaced by built-in durability. It stresses the fact that in the achievement of such objectives society will certainly not stagnate.

In the United States there is some room for optimism. Enormous billboards enumerate the millions of bottles and cans that have been recycled. Tourist notices acclaim 'Come to North Dakota and breathe air you cannot see!' Warnings against litter, not only in the towns, but in the country, threaten fines as high as $200 for one offence. There is ample evidence that the 'throw away society' is even now changing its attitude. Oddly enough, it seems that the technique of the Madison Avenue advertising agencies, whose success in persuading the public into buying anything and everything, can operate equally well in the reverse direction.

I don't suggest that the counterindustrial revolution is already under way in the USA, but I do suggest that there are visible straws in the wind. Certainly the costly wastefulness of certain research programmes is being reviewed and curtailed, and research colleagues themselves express deep concern about such lavish expenditure which is based on instrumental obsolescence.

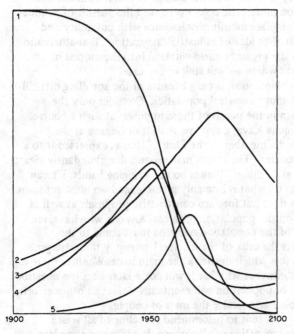

Fig 16. 1. *Natural resources*
2. *Food per capita*
3. *Population*
4. *Industrial output per capita*
5. *Pollution*

I have emphasised the point that it matters little in the long run whether the MIT group have made an error of a generation one way or the other in their predictions. What really matters is the mathematical disclosure of vitally important trends in population, natural resources, food production, industrial output and environmental pollution. These trends are unaffected by altering the input data, to whatever advantageous limits.

I would like to add my own postscript to this conclusion. In another chapter I refer to the Second Law of Thermodynamics, which states that the random element in Nature must always increase. The random element or tendency to molecular disorder is called Entropy, and every process used for the extraction of energy from the terrestrial sphere must inevitably increase Entropy, and correspondingly reduce the molecular order from which the energy was extracted. The energy of the waterfall is restored by heat from the sun, carrying the water by evaporation to the cloud cover again. Even the nuclear reactor produces atomic ash from which no further useful energy is obtainable. The point of maximum Entropy will, of course, be the point of universal thermal death, when no useful energy flow takes place between the random moving molecules as thermodynamic equilibrium. The term 'useful' is the operative word.

From the age of eighteen years, we each begin to 'age' by accumulation of Entropy, until at last the final degree of molecular order is death. The stage of universal thermal death is millions of years away, because the sun, a fusion reactor, keeps pouring out energy in the form of heat and of light quanta or photons. The latter energise the earth's 'green carpet' and, through the food it provides, our own physical bodies. The former could be utilised, albeit with greatly reduced available energy when compared with what we at present squander in the way of natural fuel resources.

As indicated, the same solar heat keeps our hydroelectric power production in action, and also causes the wind which is another valuable source of useful energy. Nevertheless, we would ultimately be industrially limited, and that point of time is really not so far off, measured in terms of man's history on the globe.

In other words, if the inescapable operation of the Law of Entropy — another name for the Second Law of Thermodynamics — could be widely realised as part of our living conditions, our choice could then lie between 'eat, drink and be merry, for tomorrow we die,' and 'eat, drink and be merry in moderation — in order that tomorrow we might still be alive.'

Whether we choose the latter or the former, could make a great deal of difference to the degree of misery and chaos that will befall the human race. Never before were the facts so evident, and never before has there been NO place in which to flee the inevitable famine.

REFERENCES

1. Pearl, R., in *Human Biology and Racial Welfare*, Cowdrey, H.K. Lewis, 1930
2. Verhulst, P.F., *Correspondence Math A Physic*, Paris, 1834
3. Calhoun, J.B., 'Population Density and Social Pathology', *Sci. Am.*, February, 1962
4. Miller, G.A., 'Information and Memory', *Sci. Am.*, Reprint, Freeman, 1956
5. Lewis, Oscar, 'The Culture of Poverty', *Sci. Am.*, October, 1966
6. Potter, van Renssalaer, *Bio-ethics*, Prentice Hall, 1971
7. Bertalanffy, L. von, *Das Weltbild der Biologie*, 1968; Weiss, P., *From Cell to Molecule in Molecular Control of Cellular Activity*, edited by J.M. Allen, New York, 1962
8. Berrill, N.H., *Man's Emerging Mind*, 1955
9. Alfven, H. & K., *Living on the Third Planet*, Freeman, 1962

READINGS

Harding, G., *Population, Evolution and Birth Control*, Freeman, 1969
Information, Sci. Am. Pub., Freeman, 1966
Davis, D., 'Urbanisation of Human Population', *Sci. Am.*, Reprint, Freeman, 1965

11. TO BE OR NOT TO BE

Soil and social destruction to rehabilitation 135 B.C. to 1948.

'Ill fares the land, to hast'ning ills a prey,
Where wealth accumulates and men decay;
Princes and lords may flourish or may fade;
A breath can make them, as a breath has made;
But a bold peasantry, their country's price,
When once destroy'd, can never be supplied.'

Oliver Goldsmith, 'The Deserted Village'.

'To plant something implies not to take something, but to produce
something. But with this Man himself becomes plant – namely a
peasant. He roots in the soil that he tends; the soul of Man discovers
a soul in the countryside, and a new earthboundness of being, a new
feeling, pronounced itself. Hostile Nature becomes friend, earth
becomes Mother Earth. Between sowing and begetting, harvest and
death, the child and the grain, a profound affinity is set up.'

Osward Spengler, *The Decline of the West*

Impact of the 1939-45 War on food production in Australia, altered
my 'taken for granted' outlook; but I am sympathetic towards my
fellow men who have not had the privilege of being thrashed by events
into a state of awareness.

This is the reason why, together with my wife, I have studied, at
three-year intervals, the progress of Land Reform and Food Production
in Italy from 1951 to 1966 inclusive.

Our investigations covered the whole of Italy exclusive of Sardinia,
and we owe a debt of gratitude to the enlightened officials of the
various Land Reform Agencies for their willing co-operation. At the
time of its inception, there was little outside interest in the progress of
Italian Land Reform.

Each geographical region has its own Land Reform administration,
its own problems, and issues its own reports. One must make frequent
visits to each region to make one's own discoveries. There is no National
Land Reform, and certainly no national publicity. There is almost a
conspiracy of silence about what is perhaps the most enlightened,
humane, rational and successful, agricultural, demographic and social
undertaking in the post-war Western world.

111

For these reasons alone, Italian Land Reform is of significance in the present environmental crisis, but when it is examined against two thousand years of abuse of arable land, it becomes a perfect example against which to measure our present situation.[1]

The story begins about 800 B.C. with the Etruscans, who appear in history as farmers working the land that they had cleared from the forest surrounding their walled towns, usually perched on some high rock outcrop for defence against other Italic tribes. They formed a loose theocratic federation of some twelve cities, not an organised nation, and their dissemination from Spina on the Adriatic near Ravenna, south into Tuscany and then into Rome and south to the Campagna, was apparently more a matter of colonising an inhabited forest region than of military conquest. Their chief cities were in Etruria, the region between the Tiber and Pisa, and it is in this region, as well as that immediately south of Rome, that their agricultural skills were so highly developed. The Apennines are very high mountains, and rainstorms are heavy, with resulting torrential run-off. The rolling, soft, volcanic tufa country favoured both erosion and swamp formation on cleared land. This the Etruscans handled with a display of brilliant engineering. They drove diversion tunnels through the sides of valleys and through ridges, creating a veritable network of drainage systems which only recently have been recognised and adequately studied. Part of the coastal region of the Maremma is today drained by the ancient Etruscan system, which, after running west along the coast, empties into the sea through an impressive cutting and tunnel through Monte Argentino. The outlet is cunningly protected from the backthrust of the sea by a breakwater cut out of the solid limestone of the cliff face.[2]

The Etruscans used bronze and then iron ploughshares, and a conservative system of two to three crop rotations adopted and used by the Romans during the early Republican period.

The Etruscan Maremma was a rich grain-exporting region, and the Federation supported a navy to protect this trade from piracy. It is the farming and soil management of these people, as well as of early Rome (which was itself partly Etruscan) that is of present interest.

The Roman farm varied in size from about six acres of rich land near a town, to 300 acres of pasture, and at the height of the Republic's agricultural prosperity it was farmed with the greatest care and skill. The usual system was alternate fallow and crop, sometimes three rotations, and always with different crops in the rotation, it being well understood at that date that monoculture was detrimental to fertility. In addition, animal and human manure was composted with straw and applied in 'well-rotted' form, according to Varro, 216 B.C., who wrote a complete treatise on agriculture. At this period, interest in agriculture was both intense and general.

112

With the growth of military conquest which followed what originally was a militia defensive activity, the situation altered. Conquest brought plunder and slaves, as well as tribute from conquered tribes. Tribute was money power for the Senate. Plunder was the reward for soldiers, and especially for generals, and slaves were the equivalent of farm tractors and machines generally.

Steadily the old virtues of a rather puritanical, closely knit family tradition, were undermined – more especially after the farms, depleted of sons, were sold to wealthy senators and war profiteers. Their great acres (*latifundia*) were worked by chain gangs of slaves under the lash of overseers, and all the patient care of the soil, the manuring, the fallow, the rotations, and the maintenance of drainage and of careful animal husbandry were more and more neglected.

This is the position as it is with us today. Instead of slaves and overseers we use machines, fuel and chemicals; instead of the farmer, who has over the years learned to know his land in its differing fields, the effects of seasonal variations, and of different rotations as well as early signs of stock troubles, we have agricultural experts and business management operating in terms of theories. Moreover, the absentee landlord is not always the equivalent of a Roman senator, but may be more often a business conglomerate, the directors of which deal with profitability of manifold subsidiaries ranging from breakfast foods to machine tools, from insurance to real estate.

The desolate, uninhabited appearance of the Maremma and the large holdings worked by foreign slaves, was noted in 140 B.C., by Tiberius Gracchus, and he vowed to rectify this state of affairs. He saw that because only landowners were permitted to serve in the army, the future of Rome would be threatened by the decay of the best Roman virtues and that Roman democracy would itself be destroyed by the rise of an unemployed, impoverished proletariat living on the dole in Rome.

On his return from Spain in 135 B.C., he offered himself for election as a Tribune of the Plebs, the rough equivalent of the Labour Party, on three issues. These were: no-one to be permitted to hold more than 333 acres of public land, purchased or rented, or, if he had two sons, 666 acres; that all such land held in larger lots be returned with compensation to the owners; that such retired land be allocated in 20-acre lots to poor citizens on condition that they could not sell the land and would pay an annual tax.

He was elected, and in his epochal oration, proposing what was in part merely the implementation of the Licinian Law of 367 B.C. he said:

'The beasts of the field and the birds of the air have their holes and hiding places, but the men who fight and die for Italy enjoy only the light and the air. Our Generals urge their men to fight for the graves and shrines of their ancestors. The appeal is idle and false. You cannot point to a paternal altar, you have no ancestral tomb, you fight and die to give luxury to others. You are called the masters of the world, but there is not a food of ground that you can call your own.'

The result was predictable. He was denounced for seeking to become a dictator and assassinated by an agent of the Senate.

Under the Empire, attempts were made to restore peasant proprietorship. The emperors were more enlightened than the Senate, dominated as it was by the large landowners. Domitian tried unsuccessfully to re-establish cereal crops in Italy – the soil deterioration had gone too far, and Italy faced starvation. Vespasian forced the Senate to accept him as Emperor by holding Egypt and the wheat supply. Septimus Severus did the same by holding North Africa. The State became the distributor of grain. Claudius had to insure shippers against loss, or risk riots due to failure of the dole of grain.

Behind the facade of lingering Roman magnificence lurked the spectre of famine due to impoverishment and the proletarianising of its peasants, and degradation of its arable land often to malarial swamp.

But in the fourth century A.D., Italy became an occupied country, and the Western Empire existed in name only, and it continued to be so until Garibaldi and Cavour reunited it. Unless one has travelled every region of the Italian peninsula, making careful observations, one cannot adequately picture the resulting destruction of its natural assets during the period.

With the opening of the Western sea routes, the powerful Italian City Republics sank into decline and Byzantines, Saracens, Austrians, French and Spaniards divided and ruled the various regions of the Peninsula. Malaria, the legacy of Roman Imperialism, now haunted the land like a spectre and drove settlers from the endemic regions. It is fascinating to review these centuries of struggle against a 'miasma', which today is under control. For example, without realising how it had happened, the rulers of Savoy largely rid Piedmont of malaria as a result of river control. This region in the eighteenth century was thus changed from an uncultivated to a populous rice-growing area.

But, in the Maremma from the seventeenth to the nineteenth century, all attempts to settle farmers in the region failed owing to the severity of malaria. Cosimo di Medici I succeeded in settling at Massa colonists from Modena and Brescia. Francesco I attempted without success, to settle Greek migrants in Sovana, and about the middle of the nineteenth century the first Grand Duke of Lorraine, Francesco II, established a nucleus of migrants from Lorraine.

Nevertheless, all these attempts to establish a peasant population in the Etruscan Maremma failed despite every inducement and privilege offered by successive rulers. The Maremma had indeed earned a sinister reputation.

Here is a description of the Tuscan Maremma in 1838.

'The desolation of the Tuscan Maremma must be attributed principally, if not entirely, to the malignancy of the air: in many cases unhealthy, in some actually fatal. Little by little, places more or less free from infection succumbed to the bad exhalations, driving away the larger part of the population. Thus the soil became deserted by man and all places of industry.'

As recently as 1910, a visitor wrote this account.

'Immediately outside Grosseto begins the Maremma. The Maremma city is like an oasis of the desert, a place of stop-over, of refuge and safety, and the beneficence disappears on leaving its walls. Crossing the Ombrone augments if possible, the squalor and desolation. Here the marshes, the waste, the abandoned are all too visible. The country is neglected without becoming wild. Everywhere is green muddy, stagnant water, everywhere yellow putrescence, which not even the ranunculi and daisies which are abundant on vast areas succeed in pitifully concealing.'

Even near Rome itself, a Papal attempt to convert rough pasture at Ostia into farm holdings failed in the nineteenth century; and in the Pontine Marshes, repeated attempts, even after the construction of the Linea Pia Canal, failed, owing to malaria, to restore the small land owners. The attempt to utilise the swampy area of the lower Tiber led to the discovery of the ruins under the fields of the once flourishing Imperial port of Ostia. They had been buried under centuries of silt deposited by the annual Tiber floods, and were not revealed until first excavated by order of Mussolini. These floods were caused by deforestation of the slopes of the Appenines, and the soil mismanagement of the landed proprietors.

The repeated attempts and failures to restore the marshes to farmlands causes one to think of historic processes in a new way. Historians pay so little attention to the mundane but basic facts of food production, that the lesson they should teach is overlooked.

Consider the migrations mentioned above, that were encouraged. Consider the fact that even today, there are ethnic pockets of Albanians and Greeks in the Volturno region North of Naples. They were introduced by a Spanish Bourbon king of Naples!

So much for the history of depletion of soil fertility in the Italian ecosphere, and the associated national decay. Now let us consider the modern sequel.

Following World War I, the Italian Government undertook the task of settling ex-soldiers on smallholdings. Two hundred and fifty thousand acres were thus converted by the Opera Nationale Combattenti (ONC); 15,000 more were made available by other State agencies; 30,000 by large-scale private enterprise; and a further 75,000 by peasant proprietors. At the same time, private development of 140,000 acres of marshland in Veneto-Emilia was undertaken. Thus the foundations of what has become the Land Reform Law of 1950 had already been laid, the drainage and settlement of the Pontine Marshes being the largest enterprise of the ONC.

In 1950 the Land Reform Law was passed and aimed at a large-scale redistribution and resettlement of the peasantry. The area involved almost one-third of the surface of Italy. The areas to be expropriated included those from which production measured against total arable production justified intervention. Appeals against expropriation were provided for, and the landowners were reimbursed in National Bonds which have increased in value since their issue.

Two-thirds of an estate were thus parcelled and the owner was required to improve his 'residual third' to the same extent as the expropriated portion. This was conducted by the agents of the Land Reform at his expense, and finally, half of the 'residual third' (one-sixth) of the whole), was expropriated against reimbursement for the cost of all improvements.

Thus the expropriated and the residual land are both brought into full productivity. The original landowners it would appear, have never 'had it so good', despite the diminution of their possessions.

Each geographical region has its own Land Reform Agency, and its own peculiar problems. In the marshes and reclaimed land of the Po Delta, drainage, desalination and large-scale rice growing precedes subdivision into smaller, intensive farm holdings. In the Fucino basin, of the Abruzzi, inefficient smallholdings were merged into larger self-sustaining units, and small industries were established. In the Maremma, both drainage and irrigation were involved, and in Puglia-Lucania-Molise large-scale provision of water supply as well as vast drainage schemes and reafforestation were undertaken.

All land was prepared by ploughing, and subsoiling where necessary, and planted to crops, vines, olives, wheat, etc. under expert agricultural supervision. The size of farm and the nature of crop was also determined on the basis of estimated productivity, and ranged from twelve to forty

116

acres. Livestock formed the basis of mixed husbandry, and the objective was self-sufficiency of the family and sale of excess produce from the farm.

Common to all these regions was the construction of Services Centres for every 20,000 acres, and hamlets for every 80-90 families. The centres are worth a visit to study the architecture alone. The hamlets have a church, junior school, dispensary and canteen and meeting place, and all are within walking distance of the farms they serve. The latter are attractive white stone and concrete buildings.

Thousands of miles of roads, power lines, water and irrigation works, formed the infra-structure. To watch the transformation of bleak, rough grazing, or malarial swamp, or eroded slopes, into a beautiful, populous countryside, has been exciting enough, but to experience the human rehabilitation has been the most rewarding experience of a lifetime.

The cost of these farms when finally allocated to successful assignees on the basis of proved ability to manage the farm for a period of three years, are subject to amortisation over a period of thirty years. The cost of infra-structure and stock and crop is absorbed by the State.

The farms remain in the family and may not be alienated therefrom, except to the Land Reform Agency. Where this does occur, the owner is reimbursed for all payments and improvements. Assignees are required to join a co-operative for buying supplies and selling their produce.

With the industrial development of Northern Italy and of Germany – the 'Economic Miracle' – the cost of living rose, and wage differentials affected the viability of the new peasant holdings.

In 1961, when the Land Reform had completed its task, this ill-effect had already been felt, and young men were migrating to industry in the North. The Government countered with the 'Green Plan' legislation, which transformed the Land Reform Agencies into Development Agencies.

While every inducement was given to industry to establish branch units in appropriate areas, steps were taken to ensure that the produce of the farms was processed in factories either newly erected, or purchased for the purpose. Instead of raw produce such as olives, grapes, wheat, sugar beet, fruit, etc. being sold to middle men, these are now converted into oil, wine, pasta, beet sugar, preserved fruit, cured tobacco, etc. and marketed under quality control by the consortia of the co-operatives which return the profits to the producer, whose economic status is thereby greatly enhanced.

These co-operatives and consortia are elected from the body of the peasant proprietors themselves. It was a revelation to witness the release of native talent in a recently propertyless land-labouring community, members of whom, if lucky, had previously some 160-80 days of work during the year.

More than 300,000 families, or rather more than a million people have been thus rehabilitated. An F.A.O. Economist report admits a 33 per cent overall increase in food production. In some farms of the Ionic Crescent, production has increased by 150 per cent.[6]

In the historic depressed region of the South, rehabilitation of the peasant extended to adult education, which of necessity had to be conducted with the utmost tact and sympathy. In this respect, the relationship between field officers of the Land Reform Agency evidenced qualities that can only be described as superb. Naturally the extent of education and training of children and youth presented a major task — consider only the training of peasants to manage their own farms, their own committees and to service their farm machinery.[7]

But the economists of Brussels have quite other ideas for Italy. Here is the announcement in the *Corriere della Sera* of Milan for 5 June 1971:

'The average production per hectare is the lowest for the countries of the EEC. Pocket handkerchief farms and archaic structure. According to the Mansholt Plan, Italy should reduce to 2 the actual 4 million rural workers. How to enlarge the dimensions of the enterprises.'

Note the use of the 'enterprise'. The emphasis is on agri-business.

What the EEC wishes to achieve is to increase profitability. A family farm, counting heads, produces less per capita. In the case of Italy, the 33 per cent increase in food production is quite overlooked. Should the Mansholt Plan for Italy become effective, 2 million peasant farmers must leave the land and live on a pension financed by the EEC. In ancient Rome they were given the dole and entertained with gladiatorial shows and chariot races — what will they be given now? Moreover, these displaced farmers must live somewhere — presumably in the countless mushrooming, high-rise apartment blocks that threaten to engulf once pleasant, ancient towns. They will become a modern counterpart of the proletariat of ancient Rome of 'Bread and Circuses', and all in the name of progress.

The long documented history of the soils and men of Italy which I have only briefly recounted has no meaning for the bureaucrats of Brussels; neither has the 'quality of life' to which a recent summit meeting of EEC countries paid lip service.

It appears that the 2,000-year-old lesson must be learned all over again. I know of no more cogent evidence of the persistence of human ecological folly, or more enlightening perspective on the environment.

Bearing in mind the pressing Italian demographic problem and the

118

hopeful outcome of Land Reform, implementation of the Mansholt Plan would appear to me to presage an ominous future for Italy, if not for Europe.

The events that preceded and followed the ill-fated efforts of the brothers Gracchus in the second century B.C. cast a long shadow down the millennium.

REFERENCES

1. Ward-Perkins, J.B., *Landscape and History in Central Italy*, Second J.L. Myres Memorial Lecture, Blackwell, Oxford, 1966
2. Harris, W., 'The Via Cassia and the Via Traiana Nova, between Bolsena and Chuisi', Papers of the British School in Rome, vol. 33 (new series 20), 1965, pp.113-32; Judson, S., and Kahane, A., 'Underground Drainage-ways in Southern Etruria and Northern Latium, vol.31 (new series 18), 1963, pp.74-99
3. Toman, R., and Miletti, R., 'La Colonizzazione nel Miglioramento delle Struttore Agrarie', *Revista Agricoltura*, Viale Reg. Margharita, Rome, 1961, pp.1-13; Tartini, F., *Memorie sul Bonificamento delle Maremme Toscane*, Firenze, Guiseppe Molini, 1838, p.484; Nicolosi, C.A., *Il Litterale Maremmano, Grosseto, Orbetello*, Instituto Ital. di Arti Grafiche, Nergamo, 1910, p.125; Baldasseroni, G., *Leopoldo II Granduca di Toscana e i Suoi Tempi*, Memorie Firenze, 1871, p.632
4. Bandini, M., 'Revista di Politica Agraria', *Edizioni Agricoli*, Bologna, 1954
5. Bufalini, B., *Pensieri intorno al Miglior modo di Studiare le Malattie di Maremma*, Antonini, Grosseto, 1845, p.95
6. F.A.O. Agricultural Study No. 53, *Land Reform in Italy: Achievements and Prospectives*, 1961, pp.29-32; Bandini, M., 'L'offensiva contro la Riforma', *Politica Agraria*, No. 2, *1956;* ibid., *'Six Years of Land Reform'*, *Quarterly Review of La Banca Nationale del Lavoro*, No. 41, 1957, Rome.
7. Stanton Hicks, C., *Land Reform in Southern Italy*, Adelaide, 1967

12. IN CONCLUSION

We human beings are in the position of one who severs the branch on which he sits, between himself and the tree. The foregoing perspectives merely encompass a view of the motivation of human destruction of the ecosystem within which we live.

The history of the antique world provides ample evidence of civilisations that have decayed as their soils were exhausted. Italy, and in particular the Maremma, provides a continuously documented story down to our present day. It demonstrates moreover the astonishing and alarming persistence of the economic beliefs that motivated the Roman Senate 2,000 years ago.

The major ecological problem is, in my opinion, the food production cycle. The re-establishment and maintenance of this cycle, is, as I see it, a matter of survival. The closing of the cycle by sewage and organic garbage composting and return to the fields could convert pollution into prosperity, provided that the fields themselves were treated as part of the biological cycle.

This, however, presupposes a fundamental change in attitude, as well as in the costs of foodstuffs, because food production under these circumstances is labour intensive.

There is no aspect of ecology so vital for the health and survival of the race as this. There is little present evidence that such thinking will prevail, because pressure of population alone, should it continue, will compel expedient recourse to exploitative rather than conservative use of land and soil.

INDEX

Printed in the United States
by Baker & Taylor Publisher Services